Authentic Worship

ORIGINALITY
IDENTITY
RESPONSIBILITY

Mark Smaw Jr.

Authentic Worship
Copyright © 2020 Mark Smaw Jr.

All rights reserved. No part of this book may be reproduced or transmitted in any form or by any means without written permission from the author.

Book Cover Designed by:
Info@innomarkgroup.com

Editing & Formatting by:
Pieces of Me Publications, LLC
Number: 419-322-0438
Email: msharmonyus@yahoo.com
Website: www.piecesofmepublications.com

Authentic Worship

Dedication

I want to dedicate this book to my mom Betty for all your prayers, support and encouragement. You know I had so many moments of frustration, disappointment, failure and worry. Through it all, you always told me things would work itself out. Even when I felt like giving up and hiding, because I was afraid. You told me to, "Get back up and do what God has called you to do." You are the epitome of a true worshipper and because of your leading by example. This is why, I'm still here to share to the world about what "Authentic Worship" really means. I love you and miss you so much. I will see you again.

Betty Louis Cox
March 24, 1949 - October 17, 2009

Table of Contents

Acknowledgements 5

Praise for Authentic Worship 8

Foreword 11

1 Authentic Worship 13

2 Eyes Wide Open 35

3 Worship Alive 59

4 Heart of Gold 77

5 In His Presence 93

6 Transparent 107

7 Benefits of God's Presence 124

8 What Are We Singing 132

9 Relevance is A Virtue 152

10 The G.O.A.T 168

About The Author 189

Resources 190

Authentic Worship

Acknowledgements

I want to thank my beautiful wife Janee Smaw for pushing me to write this book. You are the only reason why this book is in the hands of many. You have made so many sacrifices for us and our beautiful family. There are no words to describe how grateful I am to have you in my life. Only God could have done this. You constantly love, forgive, share, help, nurture and support me. You daily encourage me but ultimately, you are my favor from the Lord. I love you baby.

To my children Jazzalyn, Aniyah, Mark III and Jordyn, I am so proud and humbled to be your father. I know every one of you are a blessing from the Lord. May your lives continue to thrive, shine and influence the world. We need your unique God-given gifts, voice and character.

I want to honor my father Mark Smaw Sr. for leading me to my destiny and creating a path for me to follow. You are a great man full of integrity and humility.

I have extreme gratitude to LaToya Williams and Pieces of Me Publication Services. Thank you for believing in my vision and making this book a reality. Your compelling words reminded me that this is something I have been doing for a long time. Thank you for pouring out your expertise.

I want to thank my sister Summer Smaw for spending many hours helping me to get this book as eloquent as possible.

To Brandi Smith, I can't even begin to fathom how or why you did what you did. I want to thank you for your generosity and your willingness to obey God. Your participation played a critical role for the launching of this book.

I also want to mention Bishop Pat McKinstry for supporting all the efforts of this book. I am so blessed to have found tons of inspiration, revelation, and direction from you as a Pastor, Chief Psalmist, Author, and Worshipper.

To Mark Marella, thank you for the art work.

To Christopher Morgan of FOR MOR MEDIA thanks for the amazing photo shoot.

Authentic Worship

Also, to Mohamad of Innovative Marketing Group *(INNOMARK)* for all of the creativity and design of this book.

I am so thankful for my Authentic Worship Church family. Thank you for growing with me on this journey.

Finally, to all my family and friends who have played a significant part in my development, improvement and accomplishments, I love you all.

~Mark Smaw Jr.~

Praise for Authentic Worship

♥ Quick Thoughts and Rating: 5 stars! I can't imagine how challenging it would be to tackle the subject matter of Worship. I do know that Pastor Smaw did it with a finesse only a talented author like himself possibly could. He approaches his writings with an unapologetically, realistic delivery packed with emotion, truth and revelation! As I was reading this book, I felt his genuineness and his heart as he expounded upon the true definition of what worship is. This book completely blew my mind! It surpassed my expectations. I know it will be a blessing to the body of Christ all around the world!!!!
~Melody A. Smith, Host of "The Melody Show

"Authentic Worship" is the perfect manual for getting us back to a posture that gets God's attention. Awesome read!
-Aaron Ashe, Founder of Beauty For Ashes Entertainment Group

"Mark Smaw tackles the topic of authentic worship with a good balance of zeal, knowledge and passion. I appreciate the way he teaches and inspires the need for worship

while also clearly conveying how it can challenge us in every area of our lives. This book will teach you how to allow your time with God to grow you closer to Him through worship so He can truly change you from the inside out."
~Tamara Young founder of ArtSoul Radio
Chicago, IL

"Mark Smaw Jr. is on the leading edge of a movement by young ministry workers to re-examine how we worship. Many are coming to the realization that we have missed, (or lost) some important aspects of worship along the way. Authentic worship delivers far-reaching results in our relationship with God and others, extending out to our families, churches and communities. This book is right on time to help the next generation achieve something that is nearly extinct in our modern churches, authenticity. I enjoyed the read and the opportunity to examine my own worship in the mirror of God's Word."
~Ike LaFontaine,
Award winning composer/producer, Executive Director of LaFontaine Foundation

"Authentic Worship goes beyond the surface level of how we have come to view worship in the modern church culture. It shows us how worship defines the very essence of our being and is more than just a song that we sing. Mark Smaw Jr did an excellent job of breaking down worship to its core and he helps us to build a strong foundation that will allow our worship to flourish and bring us to a deeper and more effective connection with God."

~LaVarn Gordon, Founder and Head Creative for Ministry Matters with LaVio Worship Pastor of Destination Church, Kearneysville, WV

FOREWORD

John 4:23-24 tells us that *"the hour is coming, and is now here, when the true worshippers will worship the Father in Spirit and truth, for the Father is seeking such people to worship Him. God is a Spirit: and they that worship him must worship him in Spirit and in truth."* This book, *Authentic Worship*, reflects the very meaning of this scripture as it compels the Christian believer to first examine their personal relationship with God as well as their commitment to the body of Christ. Pastor Smaw intensely unravels the importance of pure, unrestricted and unadulterated worship to God. He expounds on the need to be in God's presence as well as the benefits we receive from His presence.

In many of our churches today, we've allowed any type of singing to take place and have watered down the music to appease the people. Pastor Smaw urges us to reevaluate what we are offering unto to God in song and calling it worship. We must have a clear understanding and knowledge when it comes to worshipping God. Knowing what we're doing when we do what we do in worship is vital to the growth and walk of faith for every Christian believer. I pray that you all are blessed and empowered by this book of wisdom and revelation.

~Bishop Pat McKinstry,
Pastor of The Worship Center of Toledo, Ohio

1

AUTHENTIC WORSHIP

<u>Authentic</u>: not false or copied, genuine, real.

<u>Worship</u>: reverent, honor and homage paid to God or sacred personage, or to any object regarded as sacred.

Quote:
True worship is coming to God in all sincerity to live for Him. In essence, it reveals how real and genuine your life is. That part of your life is precisely the evidence of authentic worship.
~Mark Smaw Jr

Now, what exactly is authentic worship? Before we can get into any kind of discussions or explanation, we will take a journey to get the full framework of what authentic worship really is. I pray you will be able to apply some patience as you read this book.

LET'S BEGIN
I think one of the most powerful conversations of Jesus' ministry was when he met the woman

at the well in Samaria. You can definitely make an argument and that is fine. Any conversation with Jesus is powerful, right? Like when He spoke to Zacchaues who was a tax collector but short in stature. Jesus told him, "I'm staying at your house." He said that right in the midst of people who did not care for Zacchaues. Let us not forget the conversation Jesus had with Nicodemus during the night when He told him he must be born again. Then, there is the conversation He had with the man at the pool of Bethesda who had an infirmity for 38 years. Jesus tells that man to take up his bed and walk. I'm pretty certain we all have our favorites and we can all make a case. Now, this conversation between Jesus and the Samaritan woman exceeds them all for several reasons.

The number one reason for sure, is Jesus had no business having a conversation with her. He knew Jews and Samaritans did not associate with each other. It never bothered Jesus one bit. Also, Jesus had no business going through Samaria. It was a custom route for Jews to go around Samaria in order to get to Galilee, but he went through Samaria anyway. Now that's bold! In this story the conversation begins with

Authentic Worship

Jesus asking her for some water. In reality, He is trying to offer her the living water. From there, it transitions into her personal life. He asked her how many husbands she has had. Then, she tells Jesus this:

"Our ancestors worshiped on this mountain, but you Jews claim that the place where we must worship is in Jerusalem."

~John 4:20 NIV

LET'S DEBATE

What did she just say? Where is all this coming from? Some would presume she is trying to avoid and negate from her personal life. I can truly agree and attest to that to some degree. Who really wants to have a conversation about personal issues or whatever problems you have going on? Especially when the issues indicate you're the culprit. I guess if it were me, I would be trying to change the entire narrative. What if I told you that maybe, she wasn't trying to avoid her issues. Maybe she was just trying to fill a void. See, it's one thing to avoid your problems because you don't want to deal with them. Sometimes you don't want to face the fact that you're the problem in the equation. It's another thing when you're actually trying to fill a void. It could be a void from guilt, hurt or rejection. The void of bad choices or of depression. It could be the void of failure or even doubt. We all have them. We all try filling those voids in our lives with things that will never solve the dilemma.

This Samaritan woman knew there really wasn't much left to say after being exposed. However, I see a woman who is trying to fill a void. For one, she has been with countless men and from one marriage to the next. Clearly, neither of her marriages were a source that could fill the void until she met this man named Jesus. She acknowledged that Jesus was on-point and she perceived he must be a prophet. The fact that she even mentioned worship adds a whole lot more to the story. If you think about her statement, it would seem as if maybe "where" to worship was a hot topic among Jews and Samaritans. She did put it out there by saying, "our ancestors worshipped on this mountain while the Jews hold true to their own belief that the place to worship God is in Jerusalem."

Authentic Worship

THE PLACE OF WORSHIP

Some are under the impression that the only place you can worship God is at church or some kind of building, facility or edifice. The Jews felt being in Jerusalem was the place to worship God in the temple. The Samaritans were under the impression that the mountains were the place to worship God. I've actually lived in the mountains at a camp resort in Wrightwood, CA. I must tell you, it is one of the most beautiful things I have ever seen. It is filled with fresh air, tall trees and snow patches covering the rocks. It's like being one with nature. Also, there's some really good people out there who are warm and inviting. I have also been fortunate to pay a visit to the Rocky Mountains in Colorado. The higher you elevate, the trees begin to look like tiny ants. God is definitely in the mountains. For me, I probably would be on the Samaritan woman's side and say worship is in the mountains. Notice what is being said in their conversation in this scripture.

"...You must be a prophet! So, tell me this: Why do our fathers worship God here on this nearby mountain, but your people teach that Jerusalem is the place where we must worship.

Which is right?" Jesus responded, "Believe me, dear woman, the time has come when you won't worship the Father on a mountain nor in Jerusalem, but in your heart."

~John 4:19-21 TPT

The Samaritans considered the Mountains. Mount Gerazim was in Samaria. The Samaritans believed this was the place to worship God. The Samaritans were forbidden to worship God in the temple amongst the Jews in Jerusalem. Can you imagine that? They weren't allowed to worship God in the temple because they were looked upon as half breeds after they had come out of slavery. The Jews would find ways to dissuade the Samaritans from going into the temple to worship. They were quite successful.

The Samaritans had to be very creative with their own place of where to worship God. So, Mount Gerazim was the place. This was the place where the leaders of Israel would stand and speak blessings. This was the place where they believed Abraham committed the sacrifice of his son Isaac unto the Lord. All of this is partially why the conversation between Jesus and the Samaritan woman was so

Authentic Worship

important. Take a look at John 4:4, "*And he must needs go through Samaria.*"

Why did Jesus have to go through Samaria? Was it to break the code of conduct? The code of conduct was, if you're a Jew, you are to never go through Samaria under any circumstance. Of course, Jesus was very radical in his approach of ministry. He was very revolutionary. He wasn't trying to prove a point that he was going to do what he wanted to do. Was He there to simply talk about the woman's issues with her past husbands? The answer is no. Jesus is not an issue inspector or a critical analyst. All of us have issues that we need to deal with. That's why the very moment the Samaritan woman talked about worship, you don't see Jesus trying to revisit her issues about the past marriages or men.

Let's just be honest. At the end of the day all of us know what our issues are. The main reason why Jesus had to go through Samaria was to talk to this woman about worship. What can be more important to talk about than worship? I know, it's a debatable question. Apparently, Jesus felt it was imperative and necessary to talk about worship to the point that he began to prophesy.

"Woman, Jesus replied, believe me, a time is coming when you will worship the Father neither on this mountain nor in Jerusalem."

~John 4:21 NIV

Well look at that. Jesus just told her you won't be worshipping the Father on this mountain or in Jerusalem. I want you to notice that the conversation is attentive to "where" worship is. What's the specific location to worship God? Is it the temple? Is it the mountain? Is it the church building that we're trying to pay off? These are legitimate questions, but the place where to worship God is irrelevant and non-existent. God isn't concerned about where you worship Him as opposed to how you worship Him. The place of worship that God is looking for is not a geographical location. The place of worship God is looking for is in your heart. Let's read this passage again.

Authentic Worship

Jesus responded, "Believe me, dear woman, the time has come when you won't worship the Father on a mountain nor in Jerusalem, but in your heart."
~John 4:21 TPT

You can worship God anywhere. If worship was strictly to the mountains and or Jerusalem that would have a lot of us in a bind. That would put limitations on worship as well as God's presence.

Remember, God isn't concerned about where you worship. He's interested in how you worship Him.

TRUE WORSHIP IS AUTHENTIC WORSHIP
"Yet a time is coming and has now come when the true worshipers will worship the Father in the Spirit and in truth, for they are the kind of worshipers the Father seeks."
~John 4:23 NIV

Jesus gives the prophetic call. He says, there's a time coming, and it's already arrived when the true worshippers will come to worship the Father in Spirit and in truth.

So, who or what is a true worshipper? What is true worship? Well, we can never assess what's true worship based on where we go to church, what songs are being sung or even how a person is looking. Let's look at this word "true." True comes from a Greek word called, alēthinos, and it means opposite to what is fictitious, counterfeit, imaginary, simulated or pretended. By definition, this is someone who is seeking to give God something that's real. Wow! Wait, there's more! That word true also means sincere. So, let's put this in perspective. When Jesus told the Samaritan woman a time is coming when true worshippers will worship the Father in spirit and in truth, He was talking about authentic worship. True and genuine worship that will be uncompromised or motivated by fake, phony, manipulative, deceitful pretense. True worship exists when the true worshippers have come in authenticity and sincerity. Take a look at these passages.

"Now, therefore, fear the LORD and serve Him in sincerity and truth; and put away the gods which your fathers served beyond the River and in Egypt, and serve the LORD."

~Joshua 24:14

Authentic Worship

"For our proud confidence is this: the testimony of our conscience, that in holiness and godly sincerity, not in fleshly wisdom but in the grace of God, we have conducted ourselves in the world, and especially toward you."
~2 Corinthians 1:12

"Wherefore, my beloved, as ye have always obeyed, not as in my presence only, but now much more in my absence, work out your own salvation with fear and trembling."
~Philippians 2:12

Sincerity is a big deal. Sincerity in all seriousness speaks of a person who is honest, integral and trustworthy. It's a person who will do all he or she can to live by the truth. Anyone who is sincere is genuinely someone who is passionate about what they're doing. Jesus gives this prophetic call to true-authentic worship. Nonetheless, I think it'll all make sense for us to go back to the origin of where worship began so we can get a deeper understanding about what Jesus was really saying.

ORIGIN OF WORSHIP

What comes to your mind when you think of worship? Maybe you're thinking about a group of people coming together singing songs of devotion: hymns, spiritual songs and congregational songs. Maybe you see droves of people by the thousands in some megachurch, stadium or arena singing praise and worship. They have smoke screens, projectors, staging lights and a big band. Surrounded by multiple guitar players, bass, drums other percussions, keyboards and a praise team. Do you think about anybody lifting their hands, bowing down on their knees, or individuals shedding tears? Well I can tell you right now, all those things are forms, expressions of worship. Yes those things play their role in worship but it really doesn't sum up what worship really is. I think you'll actually be surprised to some extent as we talk about that more in depth a few chapters later.

See, worship is a part of our nature. It's embedded in our DNA. If you think about it, we demonstrate worship all the time. We probably fail to recognize it. For instance, if you have children, I'm pretty sure you honor them when they get good grades or when

Authentic Worship

they make some major achievements like the honor roll. It deems a standing ovation, or a hug, a pat on the back. We affirm our children all the time with words like, "good job," "you are awesome," or "you are amazing." Sometimes as parents we'll bless our children with money, clothes, and maybe a car for their eighteenth birthday just because of who they are in our lives. Then we'll tell them, "You deserve it." I know for me on a personal level, I tell my daughters Jazzalyn, Aniyah, and Jordyn from the time they were born; "you're beautiful, smart, and your mommy and daddy loves you." Oh, and how often or every now and then spouses will tell each other, " you're my everything." Can you think of anything else? What about our favorite celebrities? We fantasize, idolize and verbalize their names all the time. Let's not forget the President of the United States. We're commanded to standup out of respect because of the position and office he holds. Even when the judge enters the courtroom the bailiff says, "All rise, the honorable Judge _____ presiding." Then everyone in the courtroom stands and is waiting for the Judge to say you may be seated. The list goes on and on from the Pope to the Emperor, to anyone of royalty or in the community. There's really no way around it.

Worship is just a part of who we are. It is a part of our identity. In fact, you and I were created by God to worship Him. That means to esteem, adore, love, honor, respect and cherish Him.

"Oh come let us worship and bow down; let us kneel before the Lord our maker."
~Psalm 95:6 ESV

"Let us worship at his footstool."
~Psalms 132:7
"Ascribe to the Lord the glory due his name; worship the Lord in splendor of his holiness."
~Psalm 29:2

Jesus said in *Luke 4:8* "Worship the Lord your God and serve Him only."

In order to rightfully share a little more about what worship really is, we have to circle back to its origin. Worship as we know it didn't start with us. It has been going on for a very long time. The ideal of worship has always existed but not necessarily from some of the forms and expressions of worship that I mentioned prior. See, the purpose of this book is to enlighten you about what authentic worship really is. I believe wholeheartedly, that if we can grasp this simple truth, we can experience worship before our God like never before.

In addition to all that, part of my number one goal today is to expose worship from an origin, identity and responsibility aspect. Everything in life has an origin; a place where something or someone came from. So yes, worship has an origin. Once we can solidify and understand the origin, we can discover our identity and responsibility.

Have you ever just wondered why we never heard or seen anything in scripture about Adam and Eve physically worshipping God. The bible doe's say they used different expressions of worship like lifting hands, bowing down or lifting their voices to God? Have you ever wondered if Adam and Eve ever offered that kind of worship to God? For whatever reason, the writer felt it wasn't necessary to record and write any of that. However, this is not to suggest in any way that Adam and Eve were opposed to it. Here's why

I think it was unnecessary to state any of those things to begin with. Those forms of worship may have been demonstrated. Perhaps, the main reason why it wasn't necessary for them to express these different forms of worship was because all God required of them was to obey. Maybe he just wanted them to follow through and live out His plan. Think about this for a moment. Was there a need for spiritual warfare? They didn't have to pull down strongholds, cast out devils and demons. They didn't have to intercede for each other. They were already covered and protected as long as they carried out everything God told them to do. Even as Noah, Abraham, and others-built altars as a type of worship to God, Adam and Eve didn't have to do any of that. They didn't have to go around finding wood, rocks and other utensils to make an altar as sign of worship to God. So, what is authentic worship? If you really want to know what true worship is, true worship is about living for Him. It's about offering your life in a way that's totally committed to Him and that's what we need to get back to as a body of believers. Our origin of true worship is living for Him by which we listen, obey, and follow through with what He says. When we apply ourselves and do this, we

Authentic Worship

can make such a greater achievement of fulfilling authentic worship to God.

HOW TO WORSHIP

"But the hour cometh, and now is, when the true worshippers shall worship the Father in spirit and in truth: for the Father seeketh such to worship him. God is a Spirit: and they that worship Him must worship Him in spirit and in truth."

~John 4:23-24 NIV

This verse is the key ingredient or the antidote to true authentic worship by which God only considers as true worship. The key word in the verse is "such" which denotes a persona of character, attributes and temperament that God is looking for. This is what God wants. This is what God requires. Remember, the place of worship is not as important as how to worship God. You can worship God anywhere at any time. In fact, if we can pray to God anywhere, then quite certainly we ought to be able to worship Him anywhere. How do we worship God? We worship Him in spirit and in truth.

So, what does it mean to worship God in spirit? It's going to take the Spirit of God that dwells on the inside of you to make that happen. In fact, we need His spirit in order to worship Him because God is a spirit. The Bible says,

"But ye are not in the flesh, but in the Spirit, if so be that the Spirit of God dwell in you. Now if any man have not the Spirit of Christ, he is none of his."
~Romans 8:9 KJV

Do you see that? God placed his spirit on the inside of you so that you would be able to live the life that resembles true worship. I mean what can you and I possibly do without the Holy Spirit dwelling in our lives? It's the Holy Spirit that gives us life, power, direction and instruction so that we know and understand how to live for Him. The Bible says, in Him we live, move and have our being. The Holy Spirit is responsible for all of that. So, to worship God in spirit, we have must rely on the Holy Spirit to enable us to worship Him.

Another point in worshipping God in spirit means I'm committed to the things of God. I'm committed to the spiritual things of God. I'm committed to what God cares about the most. I'm committed to what God says and what He requires. See, when Adam and Eve failed to listen and commit to what God said, they died. How did they die? Yes, Adam lived to be nine hundred and thirty years old. Adam lived a very long time, so it wasn't a physical death. His death was spiritual. Adam and Eve died spiritually.

"And the Lord God commanded the man, you are free to eat from any tree in the garden; but you must not eat from the tree of the knowledge of good and evil, for when you eat from it you will certainly die."
~Genesis 2:16-17 KJV

God was conveying to Adam and Eve that if they ate of the tree of knowledge of good and evil, they would die a spiritual death. Of course, when they failed to obey God and fell into sin, it caused a great deal of trouble for all of us. This is why, Jesus came and gave His life for us so that we can live spiritually again. Jesus said,

"I come that you might have life and that you may have it more abundantly."
~John 10:10 KJV

What was Jesus talking about? He was talking about eternal life; a spiritual life. The very moment you gave your life to God and turned away from whatever former life you had, God placed his Holy Spirit on the inside of you. You could have been a murderer, drunkard, liar, fornicator, adulterer, whoremonger, stealer, backbiter or divider. God still chose to give you power and access to the Father by which you can experience fellowship, worship and communion with the Almighty God.

"But the hour cometh, and now is, when the true worshippers shall worship the Father in spirit and in truth: for the Father seeketh such to worship him. God is a Spirit: and they that worship him must worship him in spirit and in truth."
~John 4:23-24 NIV

How do we worship God? Notice what Jesus says; *"we must worship Him in spirit and in truth."* We've covered the "in spirit" aspect. Let's look at the "in truth" part. To worship in truth means to reverence and honor God's word. We honor His word because His word is truth. When I honor and obey His word, there's a level of respect that's given. What is God's word? Well, I can tell you this. God's word is and does a plurality of things.

God's word is truth **(Psalm 119:160, John 17:17)**
God's word is light **(Psalm 119:105, 130)**
God's word is right **(Psalm 33:4)**
God's word gives life **(Matthew 4:4)**
God's word is quick and powerful **(Hebrews 4:12)**
God's word is instruction **(Romans 15:4)**
God's word produces faith **(Romans 10:17)**
God's word is a cleanser **(Psalm 119:9, John 15:3)**
God's word is pure **(Psalm 12:6)**

I assure you that there is a whole lot more to God's word. The main thing that you need to understand about worshipping God in truth is knowing and living out His word. Say this out loud with me, "knowing and living out His word. As I begin to know more of His word and what His word says, then I begin to apply myself." It's in those moments of application,

activation and administration where true worship comes into being and manifestation. It's in these moments where my life is becoming fruitful, productive and initiative. When I worship Him in truth and the truth of His words. There's an automatic blessing at your request. Read this:
"If ye abide in me, and my words abide in you, ye shall ask what ye will, and it shall be done unto you."
~John 15:7 KJV

There are automatic blessings God will release at your request when you ask Him whatever it is you desire or need. Just recognize the if condition; *"If you abide in me and my words abide in you"*. If and when you allow the truth of God's word to remain, live, and dwell in you, by obeying what His word says, you can ask God whatever you want and he said, "I will do it." There is something so wonderful about worshipping God the right way, in spirit and truth.

2

EYES WIDE OPEN

<u>Eye</u> - sight; vision: an attentive look, close observation, or watch.

Quote:
"It is simply amazing when you look at the makeup of the book of Genesis. Genesis has 50 chapters. The irony to this fact is that the first 2 chapters detail creation, but the last 48 chapters are solely about man. From the beginning the Lord had more to say about man than anything else. Man is the apple of His eye. So, it's easy to look at what you love. The eyes of the Lord have been on man from the beginning, simply because He loves us. "Could it be that the Father has always had a longing for intimacy (worship) with man?"
~**Bishop John Williams** *River of Life Church*
Toledo, Ohio

Maybe you have been curious or intrigued about this chapter since you've come across the importance of true, genuine, authentic worship. For me, I was just as curious as you when I gathered this idea. The Lord really gave me some practical truth behind this chapter, "Eyes Wide Open."

Usually for most of us, we go through life without a care in the world that somebody is watching us. We wake up, get ready for work, school and other appointments. We may have breakfast, lunch, and dinner in between. Maybe we'll take that brisk run in the neighborhood or park. For some of us, we like to start our day at the fitness center working on our abs, biceps and triceps. Then there are those who like to go out on a date to the movies or a fancy restaurant. I mean, I could really go on and on about all the different things we do. Now, did you ever consider the fact that somebody is watching you?

I just had a flashback. There's song back in the day from a group artist named The Police, who had these lyrics, "Every breath you take, every move you make, every bond you break, every step you take, I'll be watching you, every single day, every word you say, every game you play, every night you stay, I'll be watching you." Yes, these are powerful lyrics and there's truth to them.

Authentic Worship

These lyrics describe the very way that God is watching us. Oh, believe me there's a lot of truth to this idea. Let's look at a few scriptures.

"The EYES of the Lord SEARCHETH the whole earth in order to strengthen those who's fully committed to him."
~*2 Chronicles 16:9 NLT*

Well, look at God. His eyes are on us so that He can give us strength. Whenever you find a word ending in "th" it means a continuation. God isn't just looking at you one day and then he decides to take a day off so he can look at somebody else. God has his eyes on you every day, every hour, every minute, every second.

"The EYES of the Lord are in every place, beholding the evil and the good."
~*Proverbs 15:3 KJV*

Similarly, to those He watches to give strength when they need it. His eyes are also in every place. That could be your home, your office cubicle on the job and even the restroom at school. God sees everything you're doing whether good deeds or bad deeds.

"And I tell you this, you must give an account on judgment day for EVERY idle word you speak."
~Matthew 12:36 NLT

The key word in this text is "every". We have to give an account for every careless word that comes out of our mouth because somebody or is keeping record. Somebody is watching what I say and how I say it. So are my words offensive, abusive, derogative, vulgar, demeaning or are my words wholesome, encouraging, positive, and helpful? These scriptures support the idea that God is watching us. His eyes are wide open. What does God see you doing?

Now again, I want to revisit *John 4:23*. There's another nugget we need to extract and share. I believe this will give us a bigger picture of how important worship is to God. Look at what it says:

"Yet a time is coming and has now come when the *true worshipers will worship the Father in the Spirit and in truth, for they are the kind of worshipers the Father seeks."*
~John 4:23 NIV

Authentic Worship

God's eyes are wide open and He is looking for true worshippers, authentic worshippers, genuine people who have a pure love for him. He's looking for sincere believers who will keep their relationship intact with Him as their focal point. He wants people who have a disinterest to pretend but are open to giving God what He is looking for. Authentic Worship! Hallelujah!

As previously stated, God is watching us. He's a God that never sleeps nor slumbers. He is always attentive to detail and sensitive to every intricate thing that concerns us. For instance, the police look for crime and they seek to protect our communities. The dentists look to see that our teeth are clean and cavity free. They seek to make sure our teeth stay healthy and strong. Scouts are always looking for the next best athlete, that'll give their team the best chance to win. Well, what about our Heavenly Father? God himself is looking for true worshippers that will offer up sincere authentic worship to Him.

I just had another flashback. Throughout this book, you'll notice I get these flashbacks from time to time. I guess it's just a part of who I am when I get these epiphanies resonating on the inside. So, I thought about my son Mark III. He is only 5 years young and counting. He's really a handsome young man, my namesake. He's my one and only son, while I have 3 daughters that I rave about often. I just love my children. Mark III is a very adventurous type of boy. He's so imaginative, creative and just a brilliant mind. He can take socks and turn them into boxing gloves. He can take the snare stand to his drum set and turn it into a weapon. He'll go into my dresser take one of my t-shirts and turn into cape, shouting "I'm Superman, I'm Dr. Strange." He'll also take his high-hat cymbal and turn it into a shield and chant, "I'm Captain America." He will even take a drumstick and pretend it's a flute or saxophone. Where he gets all of these ideas from is beyond me. What impresses me so much about him is, he's always asking me to look and watch him do this and watch him do that. "Come here daddy, look at this!" "Look at me!" And boy, do I really get a kick out of it.

For the same reason my son calls my attention to see what he's doing, I believe true worshippers bring that same kind of attention

Authentic Worship

from our Heavenly Father. Of course, we may not tell God, "look at me," or "come see this." I think when we worship God the right way; the *John 4:23* way. God is drawn to us. He looms out of nowhere to see the true essence of worship coming out of your life. Just as I'm excited and tickled when I see my son showing me all he can do, God is excited and pleased to see a true worshipper giving Him all the glory, honor and praise. God's eyes are wide open.

WORSHIP GETS GOD'S ATTENTION
No, true worshippers don't have to flag down God to tell Him, "Look at me! Look over here;" that's unnecessary. Whenever you're living a life of true worship to God, you will get God's attention.

"Some time later Hezekiah became deathly sick. The prophet Isaiah son of Amoz paid him a visit and said, "Put your affairs in order; you're about to die—you haven't long to live." Hezekiah turned from Isaiah and faced GOD, praying: Remember, O GOD, who I am, what I've done! I've lived an honest life before you. My heart's been true and steady, I've lived to please you; lived for your

approval. And then the tears flowed. Hezekiah wept. "Isaiah was not halfway across the courtyard when the word of GOD stopped him: "Go back and tell Hezekiah, prince of my people" GOD's word, Hezekiah! From the God of your ancestor David: I've listened to your prayer and I've observed your tears. I'm going to heal you. In three days, you will walk on your own legs into The Temple of GOD. I have just added fifteen years to your life."

~2 Kings 20:1-7 (MSG)

This story is so amazing because Hezekiah the king was on his way up out of here. Could you imagine God's messenger telling you to get your house in order cause you're getting ready to die? Not sure how I would react or respond but clearly Hezekiah had enough sense to go before the Lord and pray. Prayer of course is an expression of worship because prayer is a time of conversation with God. Notice what Hezekiah says to the Lord:

- I've lived an honest life
- I've lived to please you
- I've lived for your approval

Authentic Worship

Are not all of these things the model of a true worshipper? Is this what God is looking for? Is this what God is searching for? The answer is a unanimous yes. Hezekiah reminded God how he lived for Him. Living for God is the true essence of worship. Hezekiah Lived for Him, pleased Him, and He healed him and added fifteen years to his life. God responds to the true worshipper. True worship will get God's attention anytime because that's all He's looking for. Take a look at this.

"Then Elijah said to all the people, "Come here to me." They came to him, and he repaired the altar of the Lord, which had been torn down."
~1 Kings 18:30 NIV

At the time of sacrifice, the prophet Elijah stepped forward and prayed: "Lord, the God of Abraham, Isaac and Israel, let it be known today that you are God in Israel and that I am your servant and have done all these things at your command. Answer me, Lord, answer me, so these people will know that you, Lord, are God, and that you are turning their hearts back again." Then the fire of the Lord fell and burned up the sacrifice, the wood, the stones

and the soil, and also licked up the water in the trench. When all the people saw this, they fell prostrate and cried, "The Lord —he is God! The Lord, He is God!"
~1 Kings 18:36-39 NIV

- Built an altar
- Offered a sacrifice
- Prayer
- Have done all these things at your command

Do you see what Elijah did? He built and put the altar together. So, what is an altar? The altar is a meeting place with God. Every worshipper should have a meeting place with God. That meeting place is more than a moment when the pastor is finished preaching and he or she gives the appeal for everyone to come to the altar. The altar is wherever you decide to come in God's presence. It's that meeting place when you come before God and God takes time to meet you where you are. It can be at home in your bedroom. It can be in your car on the way to work. It can even be outside at a public place. The altar is the meeting place with God. The altar is a type or symbol of worship because whenever we have

Authentic Worship

a chance to come before God, His presence is in our midst.

What else did Elijah do? He also offered up a sacrifice to God. This is very important and we'll get more into that later in the chapters to come. The main thing you need to understand about that is we must offer ourselves as a sacrifice to God. The best worship we can give God is submitting ourselves totally to him. That's the sacrifice.

The next thing Elijah does is prays to the Lord. Prayer is an expression of worship and we discussed that prior in the story of Hezekiah. Prayer is ultimately a time of devotion. It's a time when we can talk to God and God can talk with us. Your time of worship can't get any more intimate than that. Communicating, conversing and connecting with God gives Him a chance to see how much of a true worshipper you really are.

Lastly, notice what Elijah told God. *"I have done all these things at your command."* See, if you really want to be the true worshipper God is looking for, you have to obey and listen to what He says. Sometimes the things that

God tells us may not even make sense to do. Sometimes what He's telling us will require intense determination even when we don't feel like doing what He says.

After Elijah prayed, God responded to his worship by sending fire down from heaven. The fire consumed the offering and God absorbed all the water that was poured out on the altar. Authentic worship will always get God's attention.

WORSHIPPERS ARE SERVANTS
There's something very powerful amongst the story of Hezekiah and Elijah. What do they have in common? They are both worshippers and worshippers are servants of God. Say this with me, "Worshippers are servants." Yes, Worshippers are servants who serve God.

The reason why worshippers are servants of God is because you can only worship who you serve.

"The devil led him up to a high place and showed him in an instant all the kingdoms of the world. And he said to him, "I will give you all their authority and splendor; it has been

Authentic Worship

given to me, and I can give it to anyone I want to. If you worship me, it will all be yours." Jesus answered, "It is written: 'Worship the Lord your God and serve him only.'"
~Luke 4:5-8 NIV

These are the words of Jesus while he was being tempted by the devil. The devil pretty much gave Jesus a proposal. Now I have to be honest with you. The proposal didn't sound too bad. The devil offered Him all the kingdoms of the world, power, wealth and fame. Even in all of that Jesus knew what was really going on. It was about giving allegiance to the devil and I love what Jesus says because he put the devil on notice. Jesus speaks the word of God. Worship the Lord your God and serve him only. Do you see how Jesus makes the connection with worship and serve? Worshipping God and serving God goes hand-in-hand. They're totally in harmony, working together. Collectively, they both render an affinity for the things of God.

Worshipping God is solely a choice. You can't profess to be a true worshipper and you're not open to serve Him.

"No one can serve two masters. Either you will hate the one and love the other, or you will be devoted to the one and despise the other. You cannot serve both God and money".
~Matthew 6:24 NIV

You see that? Jesus said you cannot serve two masters. I know for some, we're opposed to hearing the word "slave," but the reality is we're all a slave to something. We all have to make a decision about who to worship and to serve."

"If serving the Lord seems undesirable to you, then choose for yourselves this day whom you will serve. Whether the gods your ancestors served beyond the Euphrates, or the gods of the Amorites, in whose land you are living. But as for me and my household we will serve the Lord."
~Joshua 24:15

Notice the word "choose". Worship and serving God is a choice in order to truly worship God. Oh, I love what Joshua says to the people. "As for me and my household we will serve the Lord." Joshua and his family

Authentic Worship

made the decision to serve God. You have to be willing and obedient to serve him. So, will you serve him today? Will you dedicate your whole life to him? If so, then let the true worshippers come forth. My decision is to serve Him, worship Him, and follow Him.

EYE'S ON YOU

I'm pretty certain you have the message by now. God's eyes are gazing throughout this terra firma with extreme expectation to find believers who will worship Him in spirit and in truth. Can you just imagine for a moment the eyes of the Lord are everywhere? He may be seeing all kinds of things: chaos, violence, abuse, sabotage, manipulation, false pretense, malicious acts, predators and offenders. At the same time, He can look past all those things to find you as the true authentic worshipper who pleases Him.

I'm here to tell you today that your dedication and living for God is never in vain. Don't ever doubt for one second that God doesn't see your willingness to worship and serve Him. Look at this reference of scripture.

> "Then the Lord said to Satan, "Have you considered my servant Job? There is no one on earth like him; he is blameless and upright, a man who fears God and shuns evil."
>
> ~Job 1:8 NIV

I can't recall too many conversations between God and Satan. Those kinds of conversations are far and in between. However, God speaks well of Job and he asked Satan, have you considered (thought about, paid attention to) my servant Job? For God to ask such a question would suggest that God has been paying close attention to Job. Can I tell you something? God just doesn't ask questions like this. There's plenty of people in the Bible God could give that kind of remark. Nevertheless, I think it speaks very emphatically that God's been eyeing Job's life for quite some time.

Also, there's that word again, "servant." Have you considered my servant Job? Someone who serves God. Now if God is able to share with others someone by the name of Job, and mind you, Satan wasn't the only one there in the conversation. There were angels there as well. Clearly, He always has His eye on us with anticipation to speak highly of us to His nemesis, Satan.

So why would God say something like this to Satan? Is God bragging or is He trying to hype Job up? I think ultimately there's an attraction God has with true worshippers that simply stimulates Him to a place of euphoria. Yes, God gets happy when He sees His people offering and living true worship. For God to mention Job's name to Satan and the angels, says a lot about what kind of person Job is. Do you think God speaks highly of you?

THERE'S ONLY ONE YOU
"Then the Lord said to Satan, "Have you considered my servant Job? There is no one on earth like him; he is blameless and upright, a man who fears God and shuns evil."
~Job 1:8 NIV

Now this kind of statement is saying more than a mouthful. "There is no one on earth like him." That's like us telling others, there's nobody like our God, right? Whenever you see or hear a statement like this, It can only mean the uniqueness and individuality of a person that someone else cannot duplicate, copy and plagiarize. People may try, but a counterfeit never adds up to the real thing. The real thing is God. There is no one on earth like Him. Is God trying to throw shade on everybody else? Not at all, but I do think God is trying to suggest to us that Job is somebody we need to know and learn from.

"Then the Lord said to Satan, Have you considered my servant Job? There is no one on earth like him; he is blameless and upright, a man who fears God and shuns evil."

~Job 1:8 NIV

- *Blameless*
- *Upright*
- *Fears God*
- *Shuns evil*

Are these attributes the heart of a true worshipper? Absolutely! I can never emphasize this enough. You'll see as I mention in the chapters to come, that worship is so beyond the idea of a song and the music. The life of a worshipper is much bigger than that. Lifting our hands, bowing down and lifting our voices are great expressions of worship but the soul-

Authentic Worship

centered foundation to worship is how we live for Him.

Look at what God says about Job. He's blameless. This doesn't mean Job doesn't make any mistakes, because we all do. It does mean that he walks with integrity, honesty and is upright. He's a righteous man. He fears God. Job gives God the utmost respect, reverence and dedication. He shuns evil. It means he's a person that turns away from anything that's contrary to God's will. This man Job is a true-authentic worshipper. Can God say that about you and I? It's definitely something we need to ask ourselves because God's eyes are wide open and He's looking specifically for that special unique person. I believe that true individual is you.

See, Job was so engaged with worship that he would sacrifice a burnt offering for each of his children whenever his children would come together and feast. He would do this just in case his children had sinned. Are we as parents standing in the gap for our children? Are we praying for our children? This man Job was the real deal.

HARD KNOCK LIFE

Well there's more to the story of Job and Satan didn't mind at all working out a deal to make things rather difficult and unimaginable. One thing that we all have in common is no one is exempt from trials, tests and suffering. I call it a "Hard Knock Life." The Bible says, in 2 Timothy 3:12 NIV, *"everyone who wants to live a godly life in Christ Jesus will be persecuted."*

Satan believes that some of us only worship and serve God, because of what we have. Can you believe that? Of course, it's sad to say that there are people who will only serve God, because of what they can get. Like the multitudes who followed Jesus as long He could perform miracles for them. I believe there's a body of people, a generation of true-authentic worshippers that will serve God no matter what the circumstances are. Thus, let's look at this deal Satan proposes.

"Does Job fear God for nothing?" Satan replied. *"Have you not put a hedge around him and his household and everything he has? You have blessed the work of his hands, so that his flocks and herds are spread throughout the land. But now stretch out your*

Authentic Worship

hand and strike everything he has, and he will surely curse you to your face."

~Job 1:9-11 NIV

Satan is convinced Job will curse and forsake God once everything has been taken from him and boy did Job lose a lot; might as well say everything.

"One day when Job's sons and daughters were feasting and drinking wine at the oldest brother's house, a messenger came to Job and said, "The oxen were plowing and the donkeys were grazing nearby, and the Sabeans attacked and made off with them. They put the servants to the sword, and I am the only one who has escaped to tell you!" While he was still speaking, another messenger came and said, "The fire of God fell from the heavens and burned up the sheep and the servants, and I am the only one who has escaped to tell you!"

While he was still speaking, another messenger came and said, "The Chaldeans formed three raiding parties and swept down on your camels and made off with them. They put the servants to the sword, and I am the

only one who has escaped to tell you!" While he was still speaking, yet another messenger came and said, "Your sons and daughters were feasting and drinking wine at the oldest brother's house, when suddenly a mighty wind swept in from the desert and struck the four corners of the house. It collapsed on them and they are dead, and I am the only one who has escaped to tell you!"*
~Job 1:13-19 NIV

Opposition	~	Lost
Sabeans/sword	~	Oxen and donkeys
Fire	~	Sheep
Chaldeans/sword	~	Camels
Wind	~	Children

Think about this for a moment. Look at the opposition and loss. See, every worshipper, every child of God will go through opposition and loss. This man lost his children and one thing happened right after the other. While one messenger brought bad news, another messenger was enroute to bring more bad news. I can't even imagine one thing happening right after the other. Could you still worship and serve God after all this?

Authentic Worship

"At this, Job got up and tore his robe and shaved his head. Then he fell to the ground in worship and said: "Naked I came from my mother's womb, and naked I will depart. The Lord gave and the Lord has taken away; may the name of the Lord be praised." In all this, Job did not sin by charging God with wrongdoing."
~Job 1:20-22 NIV

Job falls to the ground in worship. I'm pretty sure he had tears in his eyes. I'm sure his heart was heavy with pain, agony and maybe even defeat. Hard knock life can be so unbearable. Even in all this, Job never pointed his finger at God to blame and mind you, God was responsible for all this. God was allowing this. God could have easily denied Satan's proposal and gave Job the benefit of the doubt, but God allowed it and Job still worshipped God. He still praised God and proclaimed His goodness.

Can you worship God when everything is going wrong? Can you worship God even at the loss of family? Let me say, it's not easy at all. In fact, there's more to the story because after all was lost, God had another conversation with Satan and told him the same thing. Have you considered my servant Job? God must have really been proud of the life Job lived before the calamity and even more proud after the calamity. God is constantly watching. He's watching how we live and even how we handle opposition, challenges and tests. Hard knock life is real. Struggles are real. Pain and turmoil are real, but true authentic worship is just as real. In the midst of it all, your life is never forgotten, overlooked and under-appreciated in the middle of all of it. God's eyes are wide open and sees how you choose to worship and serve Him. God is pleased and He is proud of how you live for Him.

Authentic Worship

3

WORSHIP ALIVE

<u>Alive</u>: full of energy and spirit; lively, having life; living, existing; not dead or lifeless

Quote:
"The essence of worship is advised and even required to be in spirit and in truth which necessitates an honesty about where one's mind and heart is in relationship to God. Worship is not based on what He's done, or even what we believe Him to do, but upon who He is and our relationship with Him. We find out who God is through our experiences with Him, causing revelation to expand, therefore intensifying our desire for closeness and participation within His dealings in the earth. It is in these experiences that aren't always yielding material blessings, but offering opportunities for sacrifice and humility that we experience the liveliness of our relationship with God ... which is worship that is beating ... pounding ... pulsating ... the very purpose of God through our longing to be at one with Him in His presence. Presenting your bodies, a living sacrifice... culminating into your

reasonable service (worship). Therefore, Worship Alive is a profound idea that calls for something as lively and joyous as worship to be birthed out of sacrificial circumstances and situations."

-Pastor Michael A. McClelland
Senior Pastor and Founder, All Nations Christian Church, Newnan GA

Worship alive! Can you say that with me? Worship alive! One more time, say it with me. Worship alive! Thank you for saying that out loud and please be patient with me. There's a method to this madness. We have learned some pretty cool things about worship in the past couple chapters, but another ingredient to this recipe of authentic worship is worship ought to be alive. I believe worship has a pulse that's rhythmically connected to the heart of God. Look at it from this point of view: If Jesus came to give us life that we may have life to the fullest then everything about our worship should be lively. God's word says, "In him we live, move, and have our being." Our worship should stand out with boldness and purpose. You may ask how so? Well in the Old Testament when sacrifices had to be made and offered to the Lord for the sins of the

Authentic Worship

people, the priest would sacrifice an animal. It would be a goat or lamb but the sacrifice of the animal had to be alive. They couldn't offer up a dead animal. That animal had to be alive and breathing. In the same manner, our worship should be alive as we offer it up to the true and living God. See, anything dead ought to be buried. Let's jump into this and see what God's word says.

"Therefore, I urge you, brothers and sisters, in view of God's mercy, to offer your bodies as a LIVING SACRIFICE, holy and pleasing to God—this is your true and proper worship."
~Romans 12:1 NIV

The Apostle Paul who is the writer of this epistle is asking us to offer our bodies as a "living sacrifice." A living sacrifice is the kind of worship we should offer to God. In other words, "worship alive" give Him worship that's living, moving, breathing and deemed for His satisfaction. Jesus gave and offered His life as the ultimate sacrifice for us that we can have life and freedom from sin and death.

anything that's a sacrifice is painful. A sacrifice hurts. There isn't anything at all that's comfortable about it. The sacrifice may cost you a loss of friends because you choose to serve God. It may even hurt your feelings because there are some things you'd rather have now, when God says to wait. It could be something God is asking you to do and you don't feel like doing that. You can rest assure it'll be worth it when you look at the bigger picture, because God will see that you're living for Him and that's really what worship is all about. It's all about living for Him.

LIVING FOR HIM
With attention to this living sacrifice. It's important for us to recognize what the Apostle Paul is telling us to offer.

> *"Therefore, I urge you, brothers and sisters, in view of God's mercy, to offer your bodies as a living sacrifice, holy and pleasing to God—this is your TRUE and PROPER WORSHIP.*
> *~Romans 12:1*

To put it differently, worship is beyond the song. I'm probably raising some eyebrows on this one. Especially, for those like myself and others who lead worship in your respective churches. Let me admonish you, worship is really beyond melody, harmony and music. Although songs play a vital role in our services, worship is more than just lifting the hands and bowing down before God. Those are vital components as well, but worship is beyond that. Although, these expressions play a part in our time when we worship God, it's not the end of what true worship really is. Some people actually think that unless there's music going on and you're singing a song in church, there's no worship. In fact, those physical expressions are just scratching the surface, but true worship is much deeper than that. Worship is about living for Him and giving myself to Him. It's about how I conduct myself and treat others. Worship is How I live.

LIVE IT UP
Why not live it up? Why not live your best life? Your best life should be a life of worship that pleases Him. Notice what it says in Romans 12:1 NIV *"Therefore, I urge you, brothers and sisters, in view of God's mercy, to offer your bodies as a living sacrifice, holy and pleasing to God—this is your true and proper worship."*

Our worship should be pleasing, satisfying, and acceptable to God. There is a worship that

God is looking for. God knows what he wants and it's up to us to give Him worship that pleases Him. For example, let's look at this.

"In the course of time, Cain brought some of the fruits of the soil as an offering to the Lord. And Abel also brought an offering—fat portions from some of the firstborn of his flock. The Lord looked with favor on Abel and his offering, but on Cain and his offering he did not look with favor. So, Cain was very angry, and his face was downcast."
~Genesis 4:3-5

Seems pretty harsh that God wouldn't accept Cain's offering. I mean come on now, Cain did offer God something and God did not accept his offering. I'd probably be upset, disappointed, and angry as Cain was. You and I have to understand one thing; we can't just offer God anything and expect Him to accept it. That would be like the waiter bringing your order out and he or she gave you a medium rare steak after you told him or her you wanted your steak well done. Can you imagine the waiter or waitress telling you, "Here you go!" What would you do? You're surely right. You would tell the waiter or waitress to take this steak back and prepare it the way you requested. It's the same way with God. God doesn't have to accept just anything. He will not settle if it does not meet His expectations of what worship really is to Him. God is a holy and righteous God. He is very meticulous about what He wants.

On the other hand, God was pleased with Abel's offering because Abel offered and gave his best. He gave the firstborn and firstling of his flock. You see that? If we're going to give God the kind of worship He deserves, it should be our very best.

For that reason, all of us should be doing whatever it takes to please God. When you want to please someone, you don't mind making sacrifices. You don't mind giving that person or persons your all. Let's live it up for Him and give God our best. Your very best is what God is looking for.

PEOPLE WILL NOTICE
In chapter 2, we talked about how God's eyes are wide open. He's looking for true authentic worship, but did you know He's not the only one that's watching. Particularly, when you

think about the fact that this world is full of people who are on a quest of their own just like you. They work, go to school, tend to their families and they're all from different cultures and upbringing. These people have their eyes on you as well.

I use to have this attitude that I don't care about what people think about me. Now, I'm a little more mature and wiser, I do care. I care to think if people really see God in me. Do they really see something that's different, attractive or maybe even influential? Because whether you believe it or not, people are watching how you live.

According to 2 Corinthians 3:2-3 MSG, *"You yourselves are all the endorsement we need. Your very lives are a letter that anyone can read by just LOOKING AT YOU."*

You see that? Your life is like a letter that everyone can read as if it was a letter written with ink. People are watching your behavior, attitude, how you conduct yourself and treat others. This lifestyle of worship is a big deal. Through God's power working in you to will and to do of His good pleasure, You have

Authentic Worship

everything you need to offer the worship God wants. So, live it up my friend. Take each day, hour, minute and second to live your life for God. Let your worship be seen. Let it be heard. Your worship shouldn't go unnoticed.

LIVE OUT TRUE WORSHIP
With attention to this, it's important for us to recognize what the Apostle Paul is telling us to offer. Look at this.

"Therefore, I urge you, brothers and sisters, in view of God's mercy, to offer your bodies as a living sacrifice, holy and pleasing to God—this is your true and proper worship."
~Romans 12:1 NIV

He says to "offer your bodies." Your true and proper worship is offering your body. Say this after me, I must offer my body. Now I'm pretty certain we all can think of other things to offer God as a token of our worship. You can give God your time, talents and treasure, but the writer says to offer and give your body.

Your physical structure has a trunk full of different systems: they are, respiratory system, digestive system, muscular system, skeletal system, circulatory system, immune system, endocrine system and nervous system. Oh yes, God made all of that, and put all of those different systems of order in you. I'm talking about the very thing that God made from the dust of the ground when he said, "Let us make man in our image and our likeness," and when he made the man, he breathed into man and man became a living being." A living being with all these complex systems that was designed by God to set order. So that our bodies can function on a daily basis. Everything from your breathing, digesting, flowing of blood, to fighting off viruses and diseases he says to offer your body. Offering your body is your true and proper worship.

In addition, to offering your body as your true and proper worship. It's very interesting how God will use people to confront different situations that have us on the hinges of walking in ignorance or turning away from God. During the time when the Apostle Paul wrote this book it was a big deal, because the Romans actually thought God didn't have any care about how men treated their bodies. They actually felt you could do whatever you wanted to do with your body. So, I'm sure you

Authentic Worship

can imagine what was going on. These men were involved in all kinds of sexual acts that was contrary to the word of God. These immoral deeds were all a part of idolatry. Idolatry is much more than just falling down on their knees to some kind of statue or graven image and paying homage. No, idolatry is much bigger than that. It involved different kinds of illicit sex, and to some degree, even taking their children's lives. This is what Paul was up against. So clearly, God gave him revelation regarding how we should worship him with our bodies. Read this.

"Do you not know that your bodies are temples of the Holy Spirit, who is in you, whom you have received from God? You are not your own; you were bought at a price. Therefore, honor God with your bodies."
                ~1 Corinthians 6:19-20 NIV

The Bible says, your body is the temple (tabernacle, sanctuary) of the Holy Spirit. That simply means your body is sacred and dedicated for the purpose of what God wants. Your body is set apart for God's use and his intention by which I am to pay high regards of reverence.

I just had another flashback. I was thinking about when I was a child between 9-10 years young. My father was pastoring Greater Grace Apostolic Temple in Toledo, Ohio and I have to tell you, my father was a great pastor. He was very old school. A fire and brimstone, holiness or hell kind of preacher. A few things my father and leaders of the church would not allow was any kind of running and playing in the sanctuary.

One story I recall was on a Sunday morning after church. A friend of mine and I were running around the sanctuary and chasing each other after church. I guess for me, I had gotten tired and I decided I would hide underneath one of the pews. Do you know my father came out of nowhere threatening me while kicking and yelling, "Get out from under there! This is God's house! We don't play in here!" Of course back then, as far as parenting people were much more hands-on than they are today, and it didn't help at all that my father just bought me the new suit I was wearing. Oh, he was very upset. Those were learning curves.

Authentic Worship

We weren't even allowed to just run around and get on the instruments. If we did, the leaders and deacons would run us right off those instruments and tell us we were not welcome. The instruments are sacred for ministry. I even recall a time I brought one of my friends to church and I was talking way too much while service was going on. My grandmother came out of the pulpit, came to my row and grabbed my hand, pulling me away from my friend and sat me in the front row. Talk about being humiliated. But when I look back now, it was necessary. These are the kind of things the church took seriously. The sanctuary at the church was a physical temple.

We, as children of God have a spiritual temple (house, sanctuary) that should be revered. God is very concerned about how we treat our bodies and he wants us to honor and worship Him with our bodies. I know we live in a society where people feel like they can do whatever they want to do with their bodies. They can alter their body with modifications. They can consume and smoke whatever they want but God's word is true. His word stands forever. He is requiring us to live a life of worship that will meet His expectations. God expects us to live a life of worship that is holy, acceptable and pleasing to Him. What could be a better way of giving God true worship, other than offering our bodies to him? He made us and created us to worship Him. Let's continue to honor the Lord with our bodies.

Jesus Christ, who is the G.O.A.T (The Greatest of All Time), was our greatest example. He offered his body as a token of worship. Look at what he says.

"No man takes my life from me, I give it up willingly."
~John 10:18 NIV

Jesus was trying to tell us then that he was committed to giving up his life so that we can have eternal life. He was willing to sacrifice his body, his time, his effort and will. Remember, before he went to the cross, he prayed three times to the Father that this cup of suffering would pass on and not last. I mean, let's be honest, who wants to sacrifice their body for someone else? However, that's what Jesus did. He offered up his body for us. He honored his Heavenly Father by giving up His body. How much more for us who have been redeemed, blood washed and set apart for his

Authentic Worship

purpose? The least we can do is give Him true worship by offering our bodies to the Lord.

"Therefore, I urge you, brothers and sisters, in view of God's mercy, to offer your bodies as a living sacrifice, holy and pleasing to God—this is your true and proper worship."
~Romans 12:1-2 NIV

One of the things I love about the word of God is how it all connects. Romans 12:1 is pretty much a pick-up from John 4:24.

John 4:24 tells us how we must worship God in spirit and in truth, right? Well Romans 12:1 tells us the proper and true way to worship God and that is to present ourselves (our bodies) as a living sacrifice. See, no matter how much the world says you can do what you want to do. Or, It's ok to live a double life and an alternative lifestyle. They may say, It's ok to do it because everyone else is doing it. You may even hear them say, "Just be free to do you. Look at verse 2.

RESPONSIBILITY

"Do not conform to the pattern of this world, but be ye transformed by the renewing of your mind."

~*Romans 12:2 NIV*

Did you see that? The writer says, "do not conform." This means no not shape your mind, perspective and character systematically to how the world thinks and operates. I want to be very discreet through here because I'm very aware we tend to cringe whenever we hear words such as do not or you can't do this, and you can't do that. We tend to plummet into a downward spiral of well what's the use. However, it's not so much of God telling what you can or cannot do. God desires so much for us to try things His way because He already knows what's best. He knows how much of a blessing your life will be when you settle in that true place of worship.

I'm telling you my friend, the world will tell you all kinds of things. Like, what to eat, what to wear, where to go, what to buy, and how to live. As a child of God, your only desire is to live a life that's pleasing to Him. Otherwise, you'll find yourself doing what the world does.

Authentic Worship

Now, notice what else the writer says, "Be ye transformed!"

Being transformed is a constant change through your walk and personal relationship with God. This idea is what really sets us apart from the world. Because as you continue to worship and live for God a change does take place. That's why the Bible says, if any man be in Christ, he is a new creature. Old things are passed away and behold, all things are become new. Now will this happen overnight? No, but if you spend enough time with God. He'll show you how to live for Him. Furthermore, our biggest responsibility as a true worshipper is making sure our love for God is untainted by the lust, passions, and cravings of this world.

> "Love not the world, neither the things that are in the world. If any man love the world, the love of the Father is not in him."
> ~1 John 2:15 KJV

Who do you love? It's very interesting to see how God himself created the heavens and the earth. Yet He's concerned that we love Him as opposed to what He created.

> "Who changed the truth of God into a lie, and worshipped and served the creature more than the Creator, who is blessed forever. Amen."
>
> ~Romans 1:25 KJV

God solely wants us to love Him more than anything else. Your true and proper worship is to love and serve Him. I'm not going to lie to you, there's a lot of things in this world that we can love. There are all kinds of pleasures out there; money, houses, land and popularity. Also, our friends and family. The only one who matters the most is God. Do you love him? My prayer today is that you'll love Him more than anything this world has to offer and that your love for Him will grow where there's no bounds.

4

HEART OF GOLD

<u>Heart</u>: the center of total personality, especially with reference to intuition, feeling, or emotion.

Quote:
"True worship is the most valuable commodity in God's economy."
   ~Dwayne Stewart of Pentecostal Tabernacle International Miami, Florida

There's a saying every now and then that goes around from time to time about a person who is recognized of good character. It's called, "heart of gold" or in layman's terms, "good people". This expression shares how good, noble and kind a person is. Of course, when you think of gold, you may think about something prestige or valuable. When you consider this expression in relation to worship. This is the very thing God is looking for. Remember, His "eyes are wide open" seeking for true genuine worshippers that worship Him in spirit and in truth. Now one of the interesting things about all this is that you and

I were created to worship God. There's a big difference between being created to worship God and having a heart to worship God. It's two different things. Think about it this way. Angels were created to worship God. There are angels in heaven as we speak chanting, "Holy, Holy, Holy." Now to us that may seem kind of boring, redundant, and the sounds of a broken record. But the Lord our God is Holy, and we can never give enough reverence to how sacred and holy He is. However, the problem with this is the angels He created to say "Holy, Holy, Holy" over and over again do not have hearts to worship Him. It's pretty much like a program designer who puts a system in place for the software that's provided. That software is going to continue to do the same thing over and over again, until there's an update. Does this make sense?

Having a heart to worship God is the biggest thing God wants. Look at this command.

"And you must love the Lord your God with all your heart, all your soul, all your mind, and all your strength."

~Mark 12:30

Authentic Worship

I have an understanding that I'm created to worship God, but I must have a heart that chooses to worship Him. That's what separates me from the angels God created and even people who choose to worship something or someone. You cannot worship something you do not value. Who or whatever you worship must be worthy to receive the worship you offer. Is God worthy? Is He worthy to receive your worship? If so, then there aren't any qualms or discrepancies about it. I have a heart of gold to worship God.

Let's dive a little deeper into this. I want to show why the heart is so important in relation to worship.

"Guard your heart above all else, for it determines the course of life."
~ **Proverbs 4:23**

Look, He's saying to guard your heart. Meaning to watch and pay close attention because everything you do is a reflection of what's going on from the inside. There's a song I really love by Maranda Curtis called, *Inside*. The lyrics read, "Come fill my life from the inside, from inside of me, may you delight on the inside, on the inside of me, set me on fire from the inside, from the inside of me." These are beautiful worship lyrics. This worship is an inside heart thing and only God knows when our hearts and minds are truly in the place of worship that He deserves.

"The heart is deceitful above all things, and desperately wicked: who can know it?"
~Jeremiah 17:9

Our own hearts can manipulate us right out of authentic worship. We can quickly find ourselves drifting away from the presence of God and following our own instead following and obeying Him. Think about this for a moment. Where did Adam and Eve go wrong in the Garden of Eden? I mean they had everything going for them and everything they needed was already provided. They didn't have to work for food. The ground produced everything. They could have any tree they wanted except for the tree of knowledge of good and evil. What happened? We're going to deal with this in the chapters to come but very quickly if you read the story, you'll see how easily Adam and Eve fell short in Genesis 3.

Authentic Worship

Notice in both passages the words, "above all else" and "above all things."

Whenever you see the word "above" in scripture, it's talking about a higher level, place, or something beyond. See the heart is where our thoughts, motivations, passions, wants, and cravings come from. If we're not careful enough, our hearts can be dissuaded catastrophically minimizing the true essence of real worship. So consequently, what we must do is constantly go above and beyond to that higher place to find God, love God, and worship God. Here's a scripture that supports this notion.

"Since, then, you have been raised with Christ, set your hearts on things above, where Christ is, seated at the right hand of God. Set your minds on things ABOVE, not on earthly things."
~Colossians 3:1-2 NIV

God is saying to position your heart beyond to that higher place where God is. Don't allow your heart to be overwhelmed by the cares of this world. Don't allow what's popular and trendy to dictate your love and affection for

God. Don't allow people to persuade you from things of God. Put your heart into it and give true worship. Give God everything you got.

Here's another important factor about the heart. Jesus said these words.

LIP SERVICE VS. HEART CHOICE
"This people draweth nigh to me with their lips but their HEART is far from me."
                                              ~Matthew 15:8

Uh oh, you mean to tell me I can be so far away from God? Yes, your heart can be very far away, and you'll find yourself being a distant Christian as opposed to a child of God who's all in, no matter the cost. Peter, who was one of Jesus' disciples at the time, was a lot of mouth. I mean he always had something to say. On the mount of transfiguration, Peter said, "It's good for us to be here." When Jesus asked who do you say that I am, Peter said, "Thou art the Christ the son of the living God." When Jesus said, "I have to go to Jerusalem and suffer many things," Peter rebuked Jesus and said, "be it far from you Lord." Jesus even told Peter he was going to deny him three times, Peter said, I'll never do

Authentic Worship

that. Peter talked a whole lot, but do you know when things got tight and Jesus was arrested and taken to court, the Bible says that Peter followed Him from afar off. That's a distant Christian.

See, God isn't looking so much for what you say but He is looking for more of what you do. Look at this, Jeremiah 12:2 says, *"You are always on their lips but far from their hearts."* The prophet Jeremiah was telling God the people speak well of you, but you are nowhere in the center of their hearts. Is God on your heart today? Have you made the choice to follow, love and worship Him? It has to be a heart choice. Anyone can talk a good game like they're really sold out for Jesus Christ, but God knows if your heart is really in it.

How can we worship God in spirit and truth according John 4:24 and our hearts are not genuinely fond of Him? We must have a God-fearing, sincere-loving, genuine-moving heart towards God for who He is. See, when my heart is sincere there's a connection in the spirit beyond what I may be feeling and an attachment to the knowledge and understanding of who God is and what He's done for me. What has He done for me? Well, He died on the cross for my sins while I was a sinner when He chose me first that I may choose and make Him my priority. When He could have allowed His wrath and rage to consume me, but He gave me grace that I didn't warrant or deserve. He gave me mercy against judgement. Does this make sense? Your heart has to be in the right place in order to give God real worship. "For where your treasure is, there will your heart be also" Matthew 6:21.

Now let's go back to Mark 12:30. There's something else that needs to be mentioned.

"And you must LOVE the Lord your God with all your HEART, all your soul, all your mind, and all your strength.".
~Mark 12:30

If there's anything or anyone you love, you'll worship it or that person. You don't worship anything you don't love. Anything that we worship, we idolize, salute, and give allegiance to. I'm telling you one of the things that I love is ESPN (Entertainment and Sports Programming Network). I can watch it all day

Authentic Worship

and all night. I love just about every show on there: GET UP, FIRST TAKE with Stephen A. Smith and Matt Kellerman, The JUMP, Pardon the Interruption with Tony Kornheiser and Michael Wilborn. That's not including all the different sports coverage of the NBA, NFL, MLB, NHL, tennis, UCF, boxing and golf games. I'm just in love with sports, period. It can be arm wrestling, bowling, poker or X games. I just love it. Well if I love it, then clearly there's a level of worship. I'm too fond for sports and ESPN because you don't love anything that you do not worship.

See, worshipping God is about loving God as well. It's about making God the center of everything in your life. Is God the center of everything that pertains to your life? We all have to check in and assess where we are in our relationship with God. Another thing I want you to notice in the text is, "And you must" Jesus is giving us a command to love God. Hey, wait a minute. Is Jesus trying to make us love God? The answer is no. God will not force or impose His will on you to do anything but there is a need to love God. Think about how God met every one of your needs: clothing, shelter, protection, health, transportation and education. Then on top of all that, God met your spiritual needs when He gave you the baptism of the Holy Spirit. The Holy Spirit gave you power to overcome the enemy. Oh yeah, God did so much for us and so much more. Therefore, knowing that He did so much for me by meeting every one of my needs. There's definitely a need to love Him. Do you love Him today? Do you love Him with all your heart? If there's any concern, ask God to touch your heart right now. Ask God to heal and mend whatever is broken. Ask Him to put all the right pieces back together again because,

"All things work together for the good, to them that love the Lord, and who are called according to His purpose."
~ **Romans 8:28**

HEART OF WORSHIP

In light of everything that we've shared so far in this chapter there's a man of God in the Bible who I believe was the greatest psalmist ever known to man. I would be remiss for failing to share anything about his life. This man went from being a shepherd boy tending to sheep to becoming a man and king over a

Authentic Worship

nation. God's chosen people. The children of Israel. He's a warrior, a skillful musician, a songwriter, a producer, a creative genius of instruments, a minstrel, a champion who defeated Goliath and the Philistines. A king. His name is David.

There's something very special about King David that separates him from others. Not to suggest at all that there isn't anything special about other men and women in the Bible. We all have something very unique that gives us our own individuality. However, we can definitely learn a lot of things from him in regard to the importance of authentic worship and the importance of having a heart for God.

"But now thy kingdom shall not continue: the Lord hath sought him a man after his own heart, and the Lord hath commanded him to be captain over his people, because thou hast not kept that which the Lord commanded thee."
~1 Samuel 13:14 KJV

This verse is the secret sauce that makes the true worshipper so attractive and appealing to God. Why? Because the heart of a worshipper is an individual who's chasing after the heart of God. That makes the difference. See, God isn't solely interested in the worship experience. God is eager and intrigued with the worshipper who has a priceless agenda to know and long after His heart. In essence, having a heart for God is being the man or woman after Him.

Also, I want you to notice that this verse demonstrates how intentional God is. The Lord sought Himself a man. There goes God's eyes wide open again. Specifically, focused to find somebody who's more than true enough to pursue his heart. Who's interested in being that man or woman after God's own heart? Who can attest that I'm one of those authentic worshippers God is looking for? Because He can see I have a passion for his heart.

I'm not looking for a pat on the back. I'm not looking for a position. I'm not looking to be affirmed by men. I'm only looking to see what's in the heart of God so that I might be the true authentic worshipper. You know David wasn't looking around to be the next king. David was content being a shepherd tending to the affairs and welfare of sheep. You know

Authentic Worship

there isn't anything fabulous about being a shepherd, right? I mean what could be so spectacular about hanging out in the fields with dirty sheep? Not to mention, they're not all that intelligent. They have limited vision and no ability to defend themselves. Nevertheless, no big deal with David. He was faithful; caring, providing, protecting them, and although he wasn't given an invitation or welcomed to the house when the prophet came to see who the next king would be, it didn't matter. Take a look at this.

"But the Lord said to Samuel, Do not consider his appearance or his height, for I have rejected him. The Lord does not look at the things people look at. People look at the outward appearance, but the Lord looks at the heart."
~1 Samuel 16:7 NIV

All I can say is, Wow! Now you have to keep in mind what's taken place in this story. The prophet Samuel has been sent by God to go to the house of Jesse to anoint one of his sons to be king over Israel. Jesse has presented all his sons by which every one of them have been refused by God. Can I tell you something? Whatever God has for you will be for you. It doesn't matter who may be in line first. It doesn't matter even if you're not in the house. Can you imagine how David may have felt? I'm sure he dealt with rejection. But it didn't matter because whatever God has for you will be for you. No other person or persons can take your blessing away. You may not even be in proximity of the blessing, but God knows. He knows all and he sees all who is after his heart.

Do you see how God tells Samuel do not look at his appearance or height because I have rejected him. God is not caught up with the hype like man. We tend to judge and get stuck in the mud with our limited abilities to see what and who God has chosen. God is unbothered with cosmetics, antics, and external features. God says I only see one thing and that's the heart. It's men who are impressed with looks but God is impressed of what's going on inside. Men are tickled by what they can see. God is fixed on what He discerns. Men value what they think looks successful. God honors inward progress. You can never overwhelm God's interest toward those who have a desire to know his heart.

Authentic Worship

Are you getting all this now? Do you understand the importance of being that man or woman after God's own heart? Read this.

"After removing Saul, he made David their king. God testified concerning him: 'I have found David son of Jesse, a man after my own heart; he will do everything I want him to do."
~Acts 13:22 NIV

Nobody can tell me God isn't concerned about whether or not we are after his heart. In this passage of scripture God testifies concerning David. What was God's testimony? I found David, a man after my own heart. Let me tell you something. When God testifies, it's a very big deal. When is the last time in scripture, you heard or seen God testifying? We did learn how God testified of Job with these words. "Have you considered my servant Job". That was a testimony in itself and in this passage. We see God testifying about David. "I found a man after my own heart. And, he will do everything I want him to do."

God really already knows he is a man after His heart. I pray today that you will have a heart of God. That in the course of your relationship with God you will develop the true heart of an authentic worshipper who is after God's own heart. May this scripture bless you today.

"Lord, you know everything there is to know about me. You perceive every movement of my heart and soul, and you understand my every thought before it even enters my mind. You are so intimately aware of me, Lord. You read my heart like an open book and you know all the words I'm about to speak before I even start a sentence! You know every step I will take before my journey even begins.".

~Psalms 139:1-4 TPT

5

IN HIS PRESENCE

<u>Presence</u>: a divine or supernatural spirit felt to be present

Quote:
"Worship isn't a place that you go to, such as a church building. It's a sacred place that's within you. When we truly know who our God is. Then we will know our true identity in Christ. Understanding this allows access to a divine connection with our Creator and gives us freedom to be our authentic self worshipping in spirit and in truth."

~Charles Waters Jr,
Lead Pastor iDream Church

One of the most beautiful things about worship when it's real. Hearts and minds are in tune with God to walk out His plan, we're given the privilege to be in His Presence. See real worship ushers in the realness of God. True worship ushers in the true and living God. When our worship is authentic; we can experience the true authentic presence of God. Isn't that wonderful!

I tend to get very excited whenever I'm around my parents. Sadly, to say my mother, the late Betty Cox went on to be with the Lord in October 2009. However, I'm blessed to have my father. I guess you can say I'm a chip off the old block as people put it. I pretty much walked out the same exact steps as my father. Everything from education, to preaching, teaching, pastoring, and playing the organ and piano. I even tried out for football and quit the team immediately only to find out later in my adulthood my father did the same thing, LOL (laughing out loud).

Currently, I'm thousands of miles away from him but whenever I pay a visit to see him, the feeling never gets old. I'm always full of joy being in my father's presence. In fact, I tend to be that little boy all over again whenever I'm around him. Although I've grown up to become a man, I'm like a kid in the candy store because there are just priceless moments whenever I see and hear his words. How much more, whenever we're in the presence of our heavenly Father. The Bible says, *"You make known to me the path of life; you will fill me with joy in your presence, with eternal pleasures at your right hand* **(Psalm 16:11)**.*"*

Authentic Worship

This is great privilege to know that every time I'm in God's presence, there's an abundance of joy, an everlasting pleasure and fulfillment. This is what I wake up and look forward to everyday. This is what I desire for every person to experience... Let's GO!

In summary, what really makes worship so unique is not only when I'm living for Him and walking out His plan and will for my life, but God's presence is in our midst. See, what's unfortunate about all this is everybody has failed at some point or another to recognize His presence. Let me explain.

If you look very closely in Genesis, you'll notice that Adam and Eve aren't lifting their hands. You don't see them bowing down before God. No Hallelujahs, Thank Jesus, or I love you Lord coming out of their mouths. Why is that? The thing that separates Adam and Eve from us is very simple. We offer all these different expressions of worship; kneeling or bowing down, lifting our hands, opening our mouths, singing a song, etc. See Adam and Eve were constantly in the presence of God with no restraints, boundaries and limitations. There was such a closeness and authentic presence between God and man, to the point of no need for man to offer such things that are mentioned. The only necessity to worship was to live for him. To obey him.

"Furthermore, the both of them walked closely with God by carrying out everything he said. "God blessed them and said to them, "Be fruitful and increase in number; fill the earth and subdue it. Rule over the fish in the sea and the birds in the sky and over every living creature that moves on the ground."
~Genesis 1:28 NIV

Worship wasn't a strain, a pull or struggle. It wasn't like they had to go through different steps to get in God's presence. Let's think about that for a moment. How many times while you've tried to spend some quality time with God. You had so much to go through just to get in God's presence; work, school, problems, tiredness. That's a lot of challenges to press through. However, Adam and Eve simply walked in kingdom authority. They took dominion and charge in the earth as a king-ruler and that was in full essence the totality of worship. Worship is all about living for Him.

Authentic Worship

They were in total fellowship and communion with God.

Hence, what makes our worship so unique, splendid, and creative? The answer is God's presence. It's God's presence that makes worship authentic and that's really how we can experience true worship, because when God responds with his presence. You know it's real.

A GOD-AWARENESS OF HIS PRESENCE

Have you ever been oblivious to the point you felt bad because either you failed to remember or you were just ignorant because of some lack thereof? Maybe, it was mental or spiritual. Whatever it was, you wished you had another chance to make it right or you just wanted to have that moment back. Instead, you found yourself dealing with some kind of regret or wishing you could've done better. To be honest. It happens to the best of us. This is why it's so important to be so keen, witty and sensitive as possible to the very presence of God. Please read this.

"When Jacob awoke from his sleep, he thought, "Surely the Lord is in this place, and I

was not AWARE of it." He was afraid and said, "How awesome is this place! This is none other than the house of God; this is the gate of heaven."
~*Genesis 28:16-17 NIV*

Did you see that? Jacob woke up and said he was not aware that God was here. Now mind you, Jacob was dreaming. He dreamed about a ladder that reached heaven from the earth and angels were ascending and descending on it. He was sound asleep and had no idea God was there.

Can I share something with you? I believe God is so involved with us that He desires His presence to overwhelm our thoughts, dreams, ideas and visions but the biggest factor that stands in our way is ourselves because we can lack a God awareness for His presence. When I speak of a God awareness, I'm talking about us being sensitive to the Spirit of God when God says, I want you to go in this direction. An anticipation that positions us to receive from God. An expectation of God's unveiling power in our walk with him to perform miracles.

Authentic Worship

See Jesus said "I'll never leave you nor forsake you" . God always wants to be in our presence, but the problem for some is that we've been spiritually sleeping for a good period of time. My prayer today is for every person to spiritually wake up with a God awareness for his presence. So, let's take a look at 4 factors regarding God's presence.

4 FACTORS ABOUT GOD'S PRESENCE

I thought it would be appropriate to share 4 factors about God's presence that you need to know or perhaps be reminded of. One of the things that we don't want is to not have a "God Awareness" when his presence shows up. Let me explain.

1. OMNI-PRESENCE

This simply means God is everywhere and whether we realize it or not God is there. Take a look at this scripture.

"Where can I go from your Spirit? Where can I flee from your presence? If I go up to the heavens, you are there; if I make my bed in the depths, you are there."
~Psalm 139:7-8 NIV

The highlight of this scripture is "where." Actually, where can I go, and God isn't there. The writer is saying there isn't any specific place, whether heaven high or earth below. God is everywhere.

"Who can hide in secret places so that I cannot see them?" declares the Lord. "Do not I fill heaven and earth?" declares the Lord."
~Jeremiah 23:24 NIV

God himself, proclaims that He's everywhere filling the earth and heaven. What does that mean? Well just to name a few, He's in your house, your school and your place of employment. If or when you go across seas, if you decide to launch into infinity and beyond, God is right there. The God I serve is a big God and His presence is everywhere.

2. ABIDING PRESENCE OF GOD

The abiding presence of God means that he lives within us. He chooses to make a home and place of residence with us.

"This is how we know that we live in Him and He in us: He has given us of His Spirit."
~1 John 4:13 NIV

Authentic Worship

John explains that we know He lives in us because He's given us His Spirit. The power of the Holy Spirit (His Spirit) dwells on the inside of us and the very moment you acknowledged Jesus Christ as your Lord and personal savior. His Spirit found a dwelling place in your life. Look at the next verse.

"If anyone acknowledges that Jesus is the Son of God, God LIVES IN THEM them and they in God."
~1 John 4:15 NIV

You see that! God lives in you. Oh, there's more to this.

"Do you not know that your bodies are temples of the Holy Spirit, who is IN YOU, whom you have received from God? You are not your own;"
~1 Corinthians 6:19 NIV

The word of God tells us that our physical bodies are temples (sanctuary, sacred building, a place where congregants fellowship) of the Holy Ghost.

Oh, there's more to support this idea.

"To them God has chosen to make known among the Gentiles the glorious riches of this mystery, which is Christ IN YOU, the hope of glory."
~Colossians 1:27 NIV

Look at what God has done. He's revealed to us this mystery, "Christ in you" and notice out of the passages we've read "in us", "in them" and "in you". God is trying to convey to us that His presence lives within. That's why we can tell others with conviction, Greater is He that is in us, than he that is in the world. You don't have to search anymore for God. God is already here living, breathing and moving on the inside.

3. ENDOWMENT OF HIS PRESENCE

The meaning for this is God's anointing, power, and glory is upon you. It's God's way of bestowing his favor, approval, and affirmation. Take a look at the first two kings in the Bible God chose Saul and David.

"The Spirit of the Lord will come powerfully UPON you, and you will prophesy with them;

Authentic Worship

and you will be changed into a different person. When he and his servant arrived at Gibeah, a procession of prophets met him; the Spirit of God came powerfully UPON him, and he joined in their prophesying."

~1 Samuel 10:6, 10 NIV

This text is the story of Samuel anointing Saul with oil to be the king of Israel. After he anoints him, Samuel gives him specific instructions and one thing Samuel tells Saul is the Spirit of the Lord is going to come upon you. In other words, it was God's way of showing others that His presence was upon Saul. This is what God did for us.

The Bible says, after the Holy Ghost has come upon you, you shall have power. His power is His authentic authority and presence over our lives. God favored us with His presence when He chose us to fulfill his plan. Let's look at David.

"So, he sent for him and had him brought in. He was glowing with health and had a fine appearance and handsome features. Then the Lord said, "Rise and anoint him; this is the one." Thus, Samuel took the horn of oil and *anointed him in the presence of his brothers, and from that day on the Spirit of the Lord came powerfully upon David. Samuel then went to Ramah."*

~1 Samuel 16:12-13 NIV

There it is again. God's presence is upon David after Samuel anoints him in front of his brothers. Can I tell you something? You'll never have to prove yourself to anyone for validation. When God is ready to endow you with his favor, power and presence, He'll do it Everyone will see that the hand of God is on your life. Now mind you, all this took place after Saul disobeyed God several times. See God wants to favor those with His presence who chooses to follow and obey Him. We can't give God true authentic worship without total obedience and allegiance to Him.

4. MANIFESTATION OF HIS PRESENCE

The manifestation is God revealing and responding presence of His power and glory. It's God making known to man His deeds. This is a big deal because some people can be withdrawn with such aura of disinterest,

Authentic Worship

distance, and disassociation. See, the question is, how can God do something like that? What people are lacking is a God awareness. There's a vicious diploma, but this level of God's presence is critical because this is God's way of engaging Himself to mankind. See what God wants to do is to demonstrate how powerful He really is in our lives.

-Acts 2:1-4 Day of Pentecost
 -(baptism of the Holy Spirit)
-Moses and the burning bush
-Captain of the Lord comforting JOSHUA
-Saul interrupted by God on his way to Damascus

Here's another example:

"By day the Lord went ahead of them in a pillar of cloud to guide them on their way and by night in a pillar of fire to give them light, so that they could travel by day or night. Neither the pillar of cloud by day nor the pillar of fire by night left its place in front of the people."
~*Exodus 13:21-22 NIV*

God revealed Himself to the children of Israel by a pillar of cloud during the daytime and a pillar of fire by nighttime. He never left their presence. This story took place right after the children of Israel crossed the Red Sea while seeing their enemies of Pharaoh and Egypt drown. God truly wants you to know today that He's always revealing. I believe even at this very moment while you're reading this book, He wants to reveal himself to you in ways you couldn't even imagine. The Bible says, *"Now unto him who is able to do exceeding abundantly above all we can even ask or imagine...."* There's no limits with God. There's no limit to His power. God can manifest Himself at school while you're taking an exam. He can reveal himself to you while you're punching the clock at work. He can give you an epiphany that never dawned on you. I'm telling you today my friend, God's presence will manifest in your life.

6

TRANSPARENT

Transparent: easily seen through, recognized, or detected: open; frank; candid:

Quote:
"Revealing the worst of ourselves, be it a single mistake or a habitual struggle, we open ourselves to true repentance, which brings true redemption. He honors and rewards confession, because it brings us back to the place of acknowledging him as the Lord of our life and we realign to Him a life of righteousness. What we see as shattered pieces from mistakes and choices in our life, He sees as genuine art pieces to combine into a mosaic masterpiece of His grace.."
~Harmony Bathauer.

TRANSPARENCY
One of the biggest questions God ever asked was "WHERE ARE YOU?"

"But the Lord God called to the man and said to him, where are you?" Genesis 3:9 ESV

This critical question was not a question God was unable to answer. God knew exactly where Adam was but what was God addressing?

He was addressing where Adam was spiritually. See, Adam was no longer in fellowship with God. The very moment Adam and Eve ate of the tree of knowledge of good and evil, An act of separation prompted God immediately to search for Adam. Can you guess what Adam was doing? That's right! He was hiding.

"Then the man and his wife heard the sound of the Lord God as he was walking in the garden in the cool of the day, and they hid from the Lord God among the trees of the garden."
~Genesis 3:8 NIV

Talk about how the tides have turned. How do you go from already being in his presence with no limitations? They had no restraints, no restrictions or no boundaries. Adam and Eve didn't even need the Holy Spirit as we do to have access to God. Their lives were so interwoven and interconnected with each other; yet, without bounds. They hid themselves from the presence of God among trees after what appeared to be the most notorious mistake. That put the entire world in a bind. I'm telling you, having privilege or privileges doesn't give anyone a slight edge or advantage. You must continue to be mindful, thoughtful and full of discipline or else you can easily get caught up. Before you know it, all the wonderful things that were going for you can soon be lost.

This may sound rather somber and I wish there was a way I could keep everything positively sunny which is the goal. The reality is there must be some kind of truth to this amongst us. How often when we've made mistakes, we decided to run and hide, because we just didn't want anybody to know what we did. There's a level of embarrassment while knowing so many people are aware of what you did. Well it wasn't like Adam and Eve had to face many people after their mistake. It was just them, the serpent and God who knew what happened.

See, the only problem with hiding is hiding will simply last for a moment. It can only last for so long. In fact, not even a moment or split second, because God already knows where you are. Just like he knew where Adam was. For that reason, we must learn what God is looking for. His eyes are wide open and he's looking for a group of authentic worshippers that will take the initiative of transparency and just tell God, "this is what I did." Besides, when you look closely at the story, you'll notice that the moment they realized they were naked, they did something. What did they do? Adam and Eve took fig leaves to cover themselves.

"Then the eyes of both of them were opened, and they realized they were naked; so, they sewed fig leaves together and made coverings for themselves."
~*Genesis 3:7 NIV*

How did they know to do that? They didn't go through any kind of extensive training or a 101 covering class. Anybody that's been there and done it knows you'll do anything to cover up your wrongdoing. I just had a moment. You remember how much praise I was giving my son, Mark Smaw III for his creativity and imaginary mind? Well, that same young lad had a moment. I recall an evening when it was time for him and Jordyn to go to bed. Typically, my routine is to read a book with them. Then I pray over them before they go to bed and just right before I turn the lights off. We say to each other, "Goodnight, sleep tight. Don't let the bedbugs bite, sweet dreams, love you." And off they go to get their good night's sleep. Well it was 12 a.m. in the morning and I happened to stroll by just to check on them. My eldest daughter, Jazzalyn actually brought it to my attention and she tells me, "I think little Mark is playing with his Kindle." Of course I'm saying to myself, "Not my Manny Man. Not my name sake." Certainly, he's gone to bed already or maybe he's just had a bad dream and woke up. It was neither of those things. I walk in the room and I noticed he pulls his blanket up to cover his chest. I said, "What are you doing Mark?" He replies and says, "nothing," but I noticed some illumination on his neck because his Kindle was still on and lit up. Of course, as a father I confiscated the device and I told him to go to bed and get some sleep.

I'm telling you as I left out of the bedroom, I said to myself, "Why would he lie to me and try to hide and cover up his Kindle?" It's the same way with us. No matter what efforts you try to pull together to cover up your wrong, God already knows. He's the illuminator! He can see right through us like transparency sheets. As they say, it's always better to tell the truth. God wants His people to stay transparent, honest and open even when we fall short, make mistakes and fall into sin. God knows how to cover us. He is our true covering.

"The Lord God made garments of skin for Adam and his wife and clothed them."
~Genesis 3:21 NIV

God really knows how to cover us. I know it may seem like God is interested in exposing and humiliating us when we miss the mark, but I want to dismantle that myth. That's not God's interest or desire at all. Unfortunately, we put these perspectives and theories on ourselves because we take on this job to analyze the worse. The God I serve is a loving God. He's a passionate God. He cares for His own and all He wants is for His people to remain transparent and leave the rest to Him. You are

Authentic Worship

His beloved. You are his portion and inheritance. You are God's possession and he loves you so much.

I wonder just maybe, just maybe, had Adam and Eve come clean in that moment and said, "God here I am, I messed up." Would God have given them another chance to get their lives together? Certainly, who's to say He didn't give them another chance. He did spare their lives. In contrast the order of things did turn into chaos.

Eve had to submit to Adam and travail with children. Adam could no longer just reap from whatever was grown from the ground, because the ground was cursed. He had to work from the sweat of his brow. Then to make matters worse, they were excommunicated from the Garden of Eden. They were removed from the presence of God, but God still blessed them. They were still able to maintain a peaceable life, and they lived a very long time. I tell you the truth. It pays to be transparent with God.

I want to share with you 6 principles about transparency. These are 6 principles to live by.

- TELL THE TRUTH EVEN WHEN IT HURTS

Then Joshua said to Achan, "My son, give glory to the Lord, the God of Israel, and honor him. Tell me what you have done; do not hide it from me."
~Joshua 7:19 NIV

This is a beautiful greeting. Yet underneath the tones of this statement, there's a ravishing penalty. Why? I'll tell you why. First thing is giving glory to God is more than some kind of boisterous chant of Hallelujah! Thank you, Jesus and Lord I love you! Giving glory to God is the idea of offering honor, integrity and telling the truth. Notice what he says. "Tell me what you have done; do not HIDE it from me."

There is the story of the children of Israel. They are under the leadership of Joshua, and they just recently defeated Jericho. You may remember the story. The walls of the city came tumbling down. Well the campaign was far from over. There was so much more the children of Israel were determined to conquer

Authentic Worship

and conquest. Yet, they come to this small city called Ai. The plan was to send only a few thousand as an army, because it wouldn't take much to defeat them. On the contrary, the armies of Ai had the armies of Israel on the run in fear, and the children of Israel were forced to retreat.

Therefore, Joshua went before God praying and asking why they lost the battle and God told him. Someone in your camp has sinned. Someone has stolen some possessions for themselves and they have lied. To make a long story short, Joshua confronted Achan about it. Achan tells the truth how he took silver, gold, and a robe from Babylonia and hid it under his tent.

Well the outcome didn't turn out well for Achan and his family. They were actually stoned to death and burned away, but the sin he committed was detrimental to everyone. There was no way the children of Israel would be able to move forward and defeat all their enemies with this violation that could stymie their future. Talk about taking a hit for the team. It's never a good feeling when the truth hurts others, but the truth always comes out much better. What would you rather have? The truth or a lie.

- TURN TO GOD

"Have mercy on me, O God, according to your steadfast love; according to your abundant mercy blot out my transgressions. Wash me thoroughly from my iniquity, and cleanse me from my sin!

Create in me a clean heart, O God, and renew a right spirit within me. Cast me not away from your presence, and take not your Holy Spirit from me."
~Psalms 51:1-2 10-11 ESV

This scripture is a prayer from David. Remember we talked about how great of a man he was. A shepherd, skillful musician, a warrior, songwriter, a king. He was recognized for being a man after God's own heart. A true authentic worshipper. However, David made some mistakes along the way that brought chaos and calamity to his house. He slept with a woman named Bathsheba who was married to a man named Uriah. He tried to cover up his trail of sin by putting Uriah on the frontline in

Authentic Worship

the heat of battle to be killed. An adulterer and a murderer. Let me say this really quick. A true worshipper doesn't mean you're perfect. We have all sinned and fallen short of God's glory. Things happen, but what I like about David is he didn't try to cover his own mess too long. He came clean asking God to forgive him.

He simply repents, turns to God to get it right. Repentance is simply turning away from sin and turning to God to go in the right direction. This is what made David a man after God's own heart. Look at what he says. "Create in me a clean heart" David may have made some mistakes, but he never lost sight of who to turn to when he got in trouble. If you're in any kind of place where sin has gotten a hold of you, don't try to cover your own mess. Turn to God and get it right with him. He's a forgiving God. A just God. A faithful God. Just turn away from whatever has pulled you away from God and He will put you in the right path.

- OWN YOUR MISTAKES

"For I know my transgressions, and my sin is ever before me. Against you, you only, have I

sinned and done what is evil in your sight, so that you may be justified in your words and blameless in your judgment. Behold, I was brought forth in iniquity, and in sin did my mother conceive me. Behold, you delight in truth in the inward being, and you teach me wisdom in the secret heart."

~Psalm 51:3-6 ESV

Come straight forward to God and tell Him what it is you have done. This is more of David's prayer. David didn't try to play the blame game. He actually owned up to his error. He knew he sinned against God. It wasn't against anybody else. Regardless of whoever else may have been involved. He took ownership of his loss and exposed himself to God. I mean who else would you expose yourself to? I'd rather come forward and be vulnerable with God than to hide, cover my trail, and be vulnerable with people. They can't offer me grace and another chance.

- SHARE YOUR PROCESS WITH OTHERS

Authentic Worship

"Then I will teach transgressors your ways, and sinners will return to you."
~Psalms 51:13 ESV

Becoming a true worshipper is a part of discipling others to stay on the right path. One of the most beautiful things when you look back in retrospect is your mistakes can become somebody else's success. Your journal of history can enable you to influence someone else to reach their destiny and destination. The Bible says, the way of a transgressor is hard. Well it doesn't have to be hard for others that are seemingly headed in that direction if you're willing to tell them your story. Tell somebody! Help somebody! One of your greatest teachers is your experience. Your experience can save somebody's soul.

"This is why Jesus said, But I have prayed for you Simon, that your faith fail not. And when you have TURNED back, strengthen your brothers."
~Luke 22:32 NIV

Share your testimony, journey, and story.

- EXPOSE A PART OF YOURSELF TO OTHERS

"Look at my hands and my feet. It is I myself! Touch me and see; a ghost does not have flesh and bones, as you see I have."
~Luke 24:39 NIV

This is a hard one because who's interested in exposing a part of you that's the truth? I think in general we're all afraid of the truth to some extent. I guess for Jesus it wasn't a big deal, because He had already told them before his crucifixion that the day of suffering many things would come.

Just know, when you're revealing a part of yourself, it doesn't make you weak. If you're a child of God you're not a victim of circumstance. You're victor of purpose! God always causes his people to live in victory. I know it may even appear to be as if you're vulnerable but revealing and sharing a part of your story builds character and it builds others. When Jesus appeared before His disciples after His death, they were still looking like they

Authentic Worship

were in disbelief. You thought they would have been pumped up with excitement and cheer. For Jesus told them He would be killed and raised on the third day.

Notice what he says, touch me and see;

One of the best things you can do is to allow people to see a part of how touchable you are. Yes, you're human. No, you don't have to tell everything that happened, but you can give people a glimpse of something because the circumstance just shows how resilient you are.

- REAL TESTIMONIES CAN SAVE A COMMUNITY

"Many of the Samaritans from that town believed in Him because of the woman's testimony, He told me everything I ever did. So, when the Samaritans came to Him, they urged Him to stay with them, and He stayed two days. And because of His words many more became believers."
∼*John 4:39-41 NIV*

There was a time when churches used to have what was called, "Testimony Service," a time where saints gathered together to tell what God did in their lives. Some testimonies were of healing, deliverance and financial breakthrough.

Nevertheless, it was all from God's miraculous power.

I still believe in testimonies. I believe every person who is in the church ought to share the good news of what God has done. The Bible says, "And they overcame him by the blood of the Lamb, and by the word of their testimony…"

Victory comes from God! We get all of that. There's also a victory that comes from the mouths of believers who have plenty of reasons to talk about how great God is. God is big, He is awesome, and your testimony is much bigger than the confines of 4 walls. Your testimony can save a community. The Bible says, "many Samaritans from the town believed in Jesus and many more believers came." Your testimony can start a fire. Your testimony can ignite something great. Your testimony can be the very reason why somebody decided to stop what they were

Authentic Worship

doing to find God. You have a story to tell that's just as powerful as the preacher.

Go save your city. Go save your community. Go and tell somebody about Jesus and who He is in your life.

7

BENEFITS OF GOD'S PRESENCE

<u>Benefit</u>: an advantage or profit gained from something.

Quote:
"As we worship, we draw the presence of God near to us. We create a space that invites God to yield power and provision. In worship, we create a space for God to heal, deliver, bless, and restore. The effects of our worship results in blessing for us and those around us. The presence of God is worthy. The essence of God is worthy. For God truly is worthy of all our praise. He is worthy to receive praise from every nation, from every tongue, since the beginning of existence until forevermore"
~**Nessie Moise, Director of Worship**
The Lighthouse San Jacinto

Now let's take a look back in Genesis again. We learned how Adam and Eve were already in God's presence. We've seen just based on the story, there was no need necessary for worship as we do today. They weren't bowing

Authentic Worship

down, lifting hands, singing a song to the Lord to invite his presence into their presence God was already there with them. The biggest component to true worship was obeying Him and walking out His plan. However, something terrible had happened.

"So the Lord God banished him from the Garden of Eden to work the ground from which he had been taken."
~**Genesis 3:23 NIV**

Adam and Eve were removed from the Garden of Eden where God met them and spent time with them. See the moment Adam and Eve disobeyed God and ate of the tree of knowledge of good and evil. Everything fell apart. The ground was cursed, man had to work in order to eat. The woman would travail with child and her husband will have rule over her. It really pays to obey God. This is the most critical thing God is looking for. He's looking for us to obey him, follow his lead, and do what He says with prompt obedience to Him. Well as a result of man's failure to follow Him, he had lost fellowship and communion with God. I'm telling you today, we need God's presence

Let's look at David's prayer. This prayer took place after he fell into sin and slept with Bathsheba who was another man's wife. Look at what he says,

"Do not cast me from your PRESENCE or take your Holy Spirit from me."
~Psalm 51:11 NIV

Even David realized after what he had done was so dysfunctional. He knew how bad life could be if he's not in God's presence. David had, I'm sure, many encounters with God as a shepherd tending to the sheep. During those times God spoke to him and gave David songs or what we call the psalms. Now that he's become a king things took a turn in his life after committing adultery. We'll dive a little more in this prayer of David in Chapter 6.

The thing that I want us to understand is when we fail to obey God, the essence of true worship is tainted until we get it right with God. God wants us to stay in fellowship, relationship, and communion with Him. Perhaps today you've fallen short, maybe you've made some mistakes and sin has entered in. If so, you don't have to stay in that predicament. Get it right with God. Turn to Him and ask Him to forgive you and continue to move forward in God's presence.

BENEFITS OF GOD'S PRESENCE

Let me explain the blessings of being in God's presence (Obed-Edom).

"He was not willing to take the ark of the Lord to be with him in the City of David. Instead, he took it to the house of Obed-Edom the Gittite. The ark of the Lord remained in the house of Obed-Edom the Gittite for three months, and the Lord blessed him and his entire household."

~2 Samuel 6:10-11 NIV

Obed-Edom's house was blessed because of the Ark of God. Now the Ark of God or the Ark of the Covenant represents the presence of the Lord. Realize, God made a promise of how He would bless the children of Israel as long they followed and obeyed Him. He gave them specific instructions how the Ark of God would be made. It was simply a box or chest that contained the stone tablets of The 10 Commandments. It was a box made out of wood and gold that was to be regarded as sacred and holy. This box was confined in the tabernacle where the priests would come once a year to receive atonement for the sins of the people. However, the main thing you need to know is that the Ark of God represents the presence of the Lord.

Now the only reason why the Ark of God was lodged at Obed-Edom's house for a while was because somebody had desecrated the order of how the ark was to be carried. So King David, out of fear, decided to leave the Ark of the Lord behind. Nevertheless, Obed-Edom's house was blessed, and everything connected to him; his wife, his family, his land and cattle. Everything you could think of that concerned Obed-Edom was blessed.

There's seemingly some humor to this story I think David leaving the Ark of God at Obed-Edom's was to see if anything else tragic would happen. Especially after seeing Uzzah get struck by God to death for touching the ark on their endeavors to bring the ark back to Jerusalem. However, that didn't happen. Instead, God's presence blessed Obed-Edom. Obed-Edom showed reverence for such a major responsibility and he welcomed the Ark of the Lord into his house. Of course, when

Authentic Worship

David found out how Obed-Edom's household and everything around him was blessed, he insisted to go get the Ark of God at once and bring it to Jerusalem.

See, there are blessings being in God's presence.

GOD RESPONDS WITH HIS PRESENCE

Some people actually think God isn't real, or He doesn't hear me, see me, let alone is thinking of me. I want you to know today God has you on his mind. His word says, *"I know the thoughts that I think toward you* (Jeremiah 29:11)." There's a song by Anthony Brown and Group Therapy that says, "I'm a living breathing walking talking miracle," who do you think is responsible for that? That's God all by Himself. The Bible says, *"For in Him we live, move, and have our being..."* I want you to know today that the God I serve is alive and well through His son Jesus Christ who said, "I come to give you life and that you may have life to the fullest." Come and follow me closer to see how God responds with his presence.

GOD RESPONDS TO PRAISE

"The trumpeters and musicians joined in unison to give PRAISE and thanks to the Lord. Accompanied by trumpets, cymbals and other instruments, the singers raised their voices in PRAISE to the Lord and sang: "He is good; his love endures forever." Then the temple of the Lord was filled with the CLOUD, and the priests could not perform their service because of the cloud, for the glory of the Lord filled the temple of God."

~2 Chronicles 5:13-14

After the musicians and trumpeters united together in praise saying, "He is Good," look at the manifestation of God's presence. The Lord Himself filled the temple with His glory and when He showed up, the priests had to take a backseat from their general duties. Everything stops at the point of God's presence. See, when we praise God, God will respond with his presence. I believe every church ought to be a praising church. The Bible says, *"Let everything that hath breath praise the LORD."* When we praise God, God gets excited and stirred up. God says, *"He inhabits the praises of his people."* Meaning, God will come and dwell amongst us with his presence. Consider Acts 16 when Paul and Silas were in prison.

GOD RESPONDS TO PRAYER
"When Solomon finished PRAYING, fire CAME down from heaven and CONSUMED the burnt offering and the sacrifices, and the glory of the Lord FILLED the temple. The priests could not enter the temple of the Lord because the glory of the Lord FILLED it."
~2 Chronicles 7:1-2 NIV

Look at the manifestation of God's presence. Fire came down from heaven, consumed the burnt offering sacrificed and his glory filled the temple. Now this story took place after Solomon built the temple unto the Lord. He prayed an impressive prayer I might add. You can read his prayer in 2 Chronicles 6. Nevertheless, we should never think that God doesn't hear us. He hears our prayers, supplications, and conversations with Him. The Bible says, "His ear is not heavy that it cannot hear." Yes, God hears your prayers. He hears every word you say.

8

WHAT ARE WE SINGING?

<u>Sing</u>: make musical sounds with the voice, especially words with a set tune

Quote:
"I truly believe that every believer has a responsibility of worship and communion with God. True Authentic Worshippers are atmosphere-changers, prayer-warriors, and their lifestyle represents the God that they proclaim to serve."
          ~Elder Chris Byrd Founder of True Victory Ministries, and Minister of Music at Worship Center Church Toledo, Ohio

I want to shift for a moment in this chapter because when we're asking ourselves what are we singing? We need to ask ourselves are we singing songs that God wants to hear? Ultimately, everything that we sing should be unto Him. We should be singing to Him along with everyone else during worship or even in our own personal time. Of course, there are times when certain songs demand a call to

Authentic Worship

encourage, inspire, or just a place of deep thoughts pondering whether it's about what God will do or just the awesomeness of who God is.

So, what are we singing? Are we singing songs that God wants us to sing or are we only interested in our favorites songs and what's popular? I think there are songs that are popular by demand and that's fine. I also think some songs that are traditional and some that are contemporary are all appropriate to sing. I guess what I'm trying to say is, there are all kinds of songs for us to sing. We know that every song has its place. However, there are a few things that are very important for every local church and music ministry to know.

SING WHAT GOD WANTS TO HEAR

No matter what capacity of ministry we're in, whether it's the four walls of ministry or other platforms that give us an opportunity to share the good news of Jesus Christ and his love; we should always seek to please him. We should always keep in our remembrance that everything we do is not to please others but solely God Himself. So, if we're in this pleasing God business. Then we should be singing songs that he wants to hear and not so much of what I think we should be singing.

How do We accomplish such a task? To some degree this may sound pretty impossible It's really not and here's why. The Bible says, that God inhabits the praises of his people. God dwells in the midst of praises that are going on about Him. No matter what kind of song it is, If it speaks well of and glorifies Him, then God is going to come and He will manifest His presence.

Another key component to singing songs that God wants to hear is to pray. Prayer is what develops the conversation between God and man. In addition, when you spend more than enough time in conversations with Him as a leader in your music ministry, God will give you direction as to what He wants to hear. To put it differently, as a leader you're going to have to be open and spontaneous to His leading. Remember, souls are at stake and somebody's breakthrough, healing and deliverance is one song away. As a rule of thumb, let's stay prayerful. Prayer is the key that will keep us keen and sensitive to what God wants us to sing.

SONG(S) OF THE LORD

What are we singing? With so much attention surrounding this question the obvious songs we're singing is the Songs of the Lord. Songs of the Lord? Yes, the songs of the Lord. I simply call them, "The Lord's songs." Why? Because every song that comes out of our mouths that glorify Him are His songs. In fact, the Bible says, the Lord puts songs (music, melody, composition) in our mouths. The songs of the Lord are His songs. Actually, the Bible says in Psalm 137:4 *"How shall we sing the Lord's song in a strange land?"* Oh, and mind you there are tons of songs. King David who was a skilled musician and invented instruments wrote plenty of songs that are in the book of Psalm. The Bible says Solomon wrote 1005 songs. Then you have the song of Moses. This was noted when God delivered the children of Israel from the hands of Pharaoh and the Egyptians. There are songs in the book of Isaiah as well and there are many more in the Bible. God loves music.

Isn't it funny how we try to departmentalize all this music with genres and categories? However, I think we do that because it just shows the vastness of God. God is so remarkable, infinite, and so is music. So, whether they're: traditional, contemporary, hymnal and spiritual with hints of Gospel, CCM, Country, Southern Gospel, Jazz, Classical, Pop, Rock, R&B or Hip Hop, if it's a song that gives glory to God. Then it's His music. It is the song of the Lord.

Now, when I first heard of the songs of the Lord, I was like, "what is that?" It was foreign to me, but I've learned that the songs of the Lord are his songs. They are songs that speak well of him; His power, His might, His goodness, faithfulness; love, grace, wisdom and knowledge. Can you think of some great songwriters? Let me share a few; the late Andrea Crouch, Chris Tomlin, Israel Houghton and Donald Lawrence. Next, you have musical geniuses from Hillsongs, Plantshakers, Jesus Culture and Elevation Worship. Those are just a few. Do you know through all the songwriting, God gave every one of them the songs. The Bible says,

"And he hath PUT a new song in my mouth, even praise unto our God: many shall see it, and fear, and shall trust in the Lord."

~*Psalms 40:3 KJV*

Authentic Worship

"and you GAVE me a new song, a song of praise to you. Many will see this, and they will honor and trust you, the Lord God."
                    ~Psalms 40:3 CEV

Notice the words, put and gave. That's all from God. God himself gives us the music, lyrics, and melody. So, anything we sing, are his songs. The songs of the Lord.

DEVELOP YOUR OWN SOUND

What are we singing? This will be the last time I ask this question I promise. Are you singing everyone else's music or are you singing your own music? See, I believe every church whether it's a megachurch, midsize, average or small. You ought to be singing your own music. In essence, I believe God can give every church their own sound. I believe there's a sound within the walls of every gifted believer in music for the local church. Just look at it from this point of view. Every church has its own identity with their own flow, character, temperament and need. Every church has their own unique talent, skill and expertise. So why not have your own sound and your own songs.

As we've shared prior about the Song of the Lord, sometimes there's a prophetic song that speaks directly to the local church that God will give to the worship and music leader. Sometimes there's a birth of something new that speaks about what God is doing. It could be now or something he's going to do in the future. Remember:

"And he hath PUT a new song in my mouth, even praise unto our God: many shall see it, and fear, and shall trust in the Lord."
~Psalms 40:3 KJV

If God can put a new song in our mouths, then He can definitely give every church their own unique sound that speaks specifically to that local church. Let's be honest, it's nothing like having your own. I love to sing songs from other songwriters. Yet, it's something about having ownership and being a part of what God wants to write, sing, and play through you.

Again, what are we singing? Yes, I said, I promise that would be the last time, but can you imagine God giving you music not only for the house where you fellowship but a song

Authentic Worship

that speaks universally to the entire body of Christ. God can do that, but I want you and your team to start expanding and stretching your faith. Start believing God for your own sound and your own songs. Now, it doesn't come overnight. You may have to collaborate and team up with others to get the job done but you can do it. There is a unique individualized anointing on your music ministry that can birth new songs and prophetic songs that speak to the church where you fellowship. Hallelujah! Take a look at this text.

"The Lord your God wins victory after victory and is always with you. He celebrates and sings because of you, and He will refresh your life with His love."
~Zephaniah 3:17 CEV

Did you see that? God is a singer. He sings melodies, parts, lyrics. See God is so interested in music that He's going to take time to sing over His people. You must get this my friend because God wants your church to have their own sound and you as a leader along with your team can make it happen. Pick up a pen and paper. Grab your device. Grab some kind of recorder. I don't care if it's some kind of software with a mic or something from back in the day with a cassette tape. Just start playing and singing and God will give you a song for the house. God will give you lyrics that will bless your church and He'll develop a sound that's yours.

Why this chapter? Well I'm glad you asked because knowing what you're going to sing as oppose to not knowing what you're going to sing can really change the dynamic of your worship experience. Of course, this principal can apply to any service whether traditional or contemporary, it doesn't matter. Even if it's related to a praise and worship team, choir, group, ensemble, or soloist. When you don't know what you're singing there are so many things that come into play. In fact, not knowing is just as bad as some preacher or teacher who has not prepared him or herself and the only thing someone can come up with is, "I'm just going to get a feel of the service." Or how about this on; I'm just going to open my mouth and let the Holy Spirit speak through me. Anybody that condones, promotes, and settles with that kind of behavior is out of order and I make no apologies for that. Just think about being in that moment with all the

Authentic Worship

uncertainty of not knowing and it's time to serve, perform, and deliver. Well this chapter is designed for any leader in music ministry: music director, praise/worship leader, minister of music, and choir director. This chapter is for you. I've included five things to live by as a leader in your music ministry.

PREPARATION

There's nothing far worse in music ministry than being unprepared. As a leader, you have a major responsibility. When it's all said and done, everything is a reflection of the leadership. When things have failed to go as planned, someone in leadership has to give an account. When things are consistent and succeeding there's much praise to be given because the leadership is doing their job.

So, what are we singing? It is a big question because at the end of the day, there are souls in the balance. Somebody is one word or one word in song away from giving their lives to Jesus Christ. Somebody is hurt, torn up, or maybe just in a bind and struggle. Your ability to be prepared can make a difference in somebody else's life. I know some may be thinking that's the Pastor's job to win the lost.

That's so unreasonable to put all that responsibility on one person. The Bible says, in 2 Corinthians 5:19 NIV *"And he has committed to us the message of reconciliation."* The King James Version says the ministry of reconciliation. To reconcile, means to be brought back. So consequently, we have a collective role in helping people come to Jesus Christ. With your leadership in the music ministry and your labor to prepare, Somebody is going to come in union and fellowship with Him. What a blessing you are to somebody else.

Let's take a look at this text.

"But in your hearts revere Christ as Lord. Always be PREPARED to give an answer to everyone who asks you to give the reason for the hope that you have. But do this with gentleness and respect."
~1 Peter 3:15 NIV

The word of God tells us, we should be ready to have an answer when someone asks us about why we follow Jesus Christ. As singers, musicians, and whatever leadership capacity we hold, we should always be prepared and

Authentic Worship

know what we're singing for any given service. Whether you worship on the sabbath (Saturday's), Sunday's or a midweek service like on a Wednesday/Thursday, Be prepared and know what you're going to sing. Exercising preparation every day can make a big difference.

I want you to pay attention to the word, "revere." The Bible says, to revere Christ as Lord. See, everything that we're doing is unto the Lord and not man. I'm preparing myself and preparing others because I have such a high regard for God. I have a committed and dedicated life and job to the things of God as a leader in the music ministry. So, with that being said, there's a level of excellence and professionalism I must achieve every day. If all of this is for God, then I should be giving my best as a leader from spending time to be selective of what songs will be suited for every service. I need to be teaching the music to the team. Preparation is going to take some hard work, but in the end; you'll gather the best results amongst your team. There will be an atmosphere conducive for souls to experience the authentic power and presence of God.

So again, what are we singing? How do we prepare and what does that look like?

STRATEGY

If you're going to be prepared, you have to have a strategy, plan, system and idea. A strategist is simply a visionary. A strategist looks ahead and prepares in advance for the now as well as the future for the team of the music ministry. He or she begins with devising the goals and mandates to complete those goals. A strategist also keeps everyone informed of the bigger picture.

"And the Lord answered, and said, write the VISION, and make it plain upon the tables, that he may run that readeth it."

~Habakkuk 2:2

As a visionary and strategist, you have to write things down. Write down the songs you're going to sing. You can at least have the songs written down over the next month that you know need to be practiced, rehearsed and performed.

So, here's an assignment for you. Write down the songs that are going to be sung over the

Authentic Worship

next one to two months. Stress to your team, whether praise team or choir why these songs have been selected.

Also, another thing that'll help is to partner with your pastor. Find out from him or her what they sense the Lord is saying over the next few weeks. There should definitely be a coexistence between you and the pastor. If the pastor is going to be preaching and teaching on love, then you may want to consider a theme of songs that integrate love or at least a song that contributes a portion of what the pastor will be sharing. In fact, you'll be surprised how easy his job can be to deliver the word of God when you play your part delivering it in song. When you and the pastor are on the same page and all cylinders are flowing, your music ministry will be on its way to a healthy start. Come on strategists. Let's GO!

Remember, if you fail to plan what songs are being sung for the coming weeks and months. It's going to be difficult to thrive and maintain a positive direction for the team and your local church. Strategizing is about taking things into consideration and looking ahead.

STRUCTURE

When I think of structure, I consider more of materials, resources, and parts that will enable the construction to be put together. With structure there's a lot involved: the dimensions, shape, landscape, and the tools that'll be used to create what the creator has in mind. I believe the creator is an architect and an architect has a major responsibility. If there's one false move in the blueprint, then the construction of the building by default will be in error.

So why is structure so important, when we're talking about what we are singing? The songs we are singing should have structure. See, your structure should be solid. Your structure should have a secure foundation. Here's a guide to go by. Generally, most songs have a verse, chorus, verse, chorus, vamp (this should be a visual picture). Sometimes songs will have a verse, chorus, bridge, and vamp.

As a leader of worship on a praise team, a director with a choir, and a music director with a band, when you play and sing the songs there ought to be structure. There should be a format and details in place. Your praise team shouldn't have to figure out or second-guess where you're going within the song. Why are you singing the first verse two or three times? Sounds like I'm fussing but no fussing at all; just a general observation. As praise and worship leaders, we want the congregation and audience to get familiar with what we're singing, but if it's new song, it may take two to three times singing it in order for the congregation to become familiarized with it. So, you're better off singing the verse just once as opposed to singing the same verse two to three times. While all that's going on, precious time is being wasted as well. It's one thing when God is moving, and as a leader, we have to be open. We must be spontaneous when the Holy Spirit is taking over, but until that happens, stick with a format and make it easy for everybody.

ORGANIZATION

An organization is simply a system of parts, functions, and persons that operate in their perspective places for the cause of order. The last thing you want to ever experience within your music ministry is chaos. This is why Genesis 1:1-2 is so important.

"In the beginning God created the heavens and the earth. And the earth was without FORM, and VOID; and darkness was upon the face of the deep. And the Spirit of God MOVED upon the face of the waters."

~*Genesis 1:1-2*

The earth itself was a total place of emptiness with no form, no formality, no format or structure. It was a place of ruin and confusion. So, what happened? The Spirit of God moved. Meaning God began to implement a system that would bring structure, order, and continuity to the earth. The very moment God began to move, He began to speak as well and throughout creation as He spoke. Different things began to come into existence with such organization and alignment. For instance, the greater light was for the day. The lesser light was for the night. If you continue reading, you'll discover day-by-day within a week's time, God put order, structure, and a system in place. He did this so creation and man involved could understand the importance of a systematic format. So, if God instituted organization, how much more within our music ministry as leaders should we be

Authentic Worship

interested in making sure our departments flow and operate properly.

Look at this text,

> "Let all things be done decently and in order."
> ~1 Corinthians 14:40 KJV

Now these were the words of the Apostle Paul who dealt with probably the most gifted church. They were prophesying and had the gifts of tongues. It doesn't matter how gifted or talented you are. When there's no order, structure and organization, your team will become so divided. Nothing will ever get done or achieved because there's a lack of organization.

So how does this work, when we're talking about what songs we are singing? Well, if you really want to be organized, you have to categorize and put your list of songs together. When you categorize, this is what it can potentially look like. Start with a few different themes. Maybe you have some services that are annually going on all the time. That's another way to categorize and jot your songs down. For those of you who want to keep things simple, you can write your songs out on paper. If you're heavily into technology and most of us are I think any app or software will suffice. You can use Dropbox, Google reader or the Apple app called Pages (for those of you who are heavily pro apple). Whatever you do, at all costs, please document dates the songs were sung. The last thing you want is to be singing the same song over and over again. Make sure to keep track how many times you sung a certain song because after a while, it's time to sing something new and fresh.

PRAYER
Everything should be operated and done through prayer. Prayer keeps the line of communication open for God to speak while we listen to what he wants. Of course, we know as a strategist, there's a vision for the overall picture. Then there's vision week after week for every service, but prayer keeps us in tune with God. Therefore, we can learn what he wants us to sing.

"Never stop praying."
~1 Thessalonians 5:17 NLT

Authentic Worship

"Now Jesus was telling the disciples a parable to make the point that at all times they ought to pray and not give up and lose heart,"
~Luke 18:1 AMP

Prayer is a non-stop way of living. If prayer is essential for our personal lives. Then prayer is definitely essential for those who are leading worship and responsible for the choice of songs. Let's continue to stay in tune through prayer.

9

RELEVANCE IS A VIRTUE

<u>Relevance</u>: the condition of being relevant, or connected with the matter at hand: the quality or state of being closely connected or appropriate.

Quote:
"True worship requires you to be responsible to the cross vertically and horizontally. If there is no vertical connection to God, there will be no horizontal relevance to the world."

~*Bishop Nolan G. White D.D.*
The Ark of Toledo

This chapter is designed for those that lead or serve in any capacity of the music ministry. Specifically, for singers and musicians who play a vital role within the worship services. But I feel it's also necessary to share that this chapter is pretty much for anyone who has a heart for ministry. There is pertinent information that everyone in ministry, as well as the church, needs to be cognizant of.

Authentic Worship

With that being said, you know as well as I do, that every worship service, no matter what day it is, will be critical for so many reasons. There is so many different dynamics that are happening. From hospitality, welcomes, offering, general announcements, the guests, the person delivering the word of God and the invitation for people who want to give their lives to Jesus Christ. Then you have people behind the scenes who go unnoticed.

However, the biggest thing that we need to know as worship leaders is that we all have the responsibility to lead God's people into the presence of the Lord and we can achieve that as long as we're relevant.

CONNECTED AND SENSITIVE

What's the big deal about being relevant? Well, being relevant allows you to have multiple opportunities. For one, it'll keep people interested in what's going on within the service. Think about this for a moment. Many stars, artists, and celebrities seek all the time to be relevant. Everything from branding themselves, their product, to keeping their social media platforms loaded with posts of content and pictures. They strive to stay connected to the fans and their fans are always wanting to know who and what their favorite celebs are doing.

How much more for those who have such a sacred call to lead God's people in worship? See, when you look at the life of Jesus, He was very relevant. In fact, He was so relevant that even you and I strive to be like Him every day. Isn't that interesting? Even today his life is the most controversial story ever told because some say He was just a mere man like us. Some say He was just a prophet, but He is more than that. He is the visible manifestation of God as Lord, Savior, and King. In fact, He died and rose again. Believe that!

Nevertheless, observing His life He was definitely relevant. I think one of the things that made Him so relevant was His ability to engage with everyone. It didn't matter who it was or what their background and ethnicity was. He would just engage and start a conversation. He was unapologetically nervy. This man would rebuke the Scribes and Pharisees who knew the Torah and He called them vipers. He spent time with his disciples and told them stories to reveal a divine

Authentic Worship

principal. Then there were others who had ailments, opposition and challenges. He would heal them and liberate them. Needless to say, like society, He wasn't looking for acceptance. You know we tend to feel a certain kind of way when we don't get a lot of likes and attention on our page or posts, but Jesus wasn't interested in acceptance. After Jesus would perform a miracle, He would tell that person not to tell anybody what happened, because He was only concerned about pleasing His Father.

Why am I saying all this? As a worship leader, you need to understand that the people you are leading into the presence of God are in need of something from God. We all need something from God, deliverance, a breakthrough, healing and more. This is why, the Bible tells us to *"come boldly before the throne of grace that we may obtain mercy and find help in the time of need (Hebrews 4:16)."* So, as the people are coming to the house of God to worship Him, how will you engage with them? Will you tear them down and scold them because they're not responding the way you think they should. I've seen plenty of worship leaders engage from a place of fury, frustration, and confusion. They said statements like, "How can you just sit there and not give God the praise?" Or "I'll praise him by myself," "Come on now," "Maybe God hasn't done anything for you." Those kind of statements can be very harmful to the worship service and to people that are in need of a breakthrough and healing. On the contrary, whenever Jesus engaged with people that were in need, He showed them love and built their confidence. That's what we're supposed to do. As a worshipper leader, your job is to build their faith and give them hope as we lead people into His presence. We have to trust God as we sing unto Him and allow the songs to minister and serve the people. Does this make sense?

Now being relevant doesn't mean it's because your team sings the latest songs or the top 25 songs on the CCM and Gospel charts. Being relevant doesn't even mean it's because you have all the fancy technology: smoke machines, stage lights, and projector screens. I mean very personally; I like those things. They do add to the worship experience but the key to being relevant is staying connected to God and sensitive to the people you lead in

Authentic Worship

worship. Remember, these our God's people, not yours. So, we have no authority, power, or right to badger God's people. They come to worship him.

Furthermore, there is a "CROSS" dynamic or paradigm to every worship leader who leads the people into His presence. I would like to share something. It's going to be very important for you to grasp this concept as you engage with the people as a leader.

"Jesus said, if any man will come after me, let him deny himself, and take up his cross and follow me."
~Matthew 16:24

I need you to hang in there with me as I share this truth. There's been a lot of debate of the cross that Jesus carried. Some say Jesus carried only the patibulum, which is the cross bar. Others say he carried the entire cross which is the patibulum and the stipe. The stipe is the vertical bar as well. However, that's neither here nor there. The main thing to know is he carried the cross for our sins.

Now we talked about the key to being relevant as a worship leader is to stay connected to God and sensitive to the people. Say that with me. "Stay connected to God and sensitive to the people." Take a look at this illustration.

Authentic Worship

Stipe
Your connection and an established relationship with God.

Patibulum
By which we are sensitive to everyone around us.

YOUR RESPONSIBILITY TO THE CROSS

There are 2 components (see the diagram on the previous page) to this cross demonstration that I want you to see. As a worship leader because this is your responsibility. In general, we know the cross represents suffering. Ultimately, the cross was committed to those who were accused and found guilty of whatever charges during the days of Roman rulership. However, there's a cross approach we can apply through the life of Jesus as worship leaders. It will enable us to be the best followers and leaders as we endeavor to lead God's people into His presence.

The first component is the patibulum which is the cross (horizontal bar). This part of the cross represents our responsibility to become sensitive to the people. So we can sense in the spirit their weights, issues, struggles or whatever burdens they may carry. This is what Jesus did for us. He carried our sins. He carried all of our deep and dark places of bondage so that we could be liberated and walk as children of light (Isaiah 53:4 and Peter 2:24). As a worship leader when I'm sensitive to the needs of the people. I can approach with a strategy as I sing unto the Lord. It may be a

Authentic Worship

prophetic song, or it may be a song that we've sang in the past. A song that will help carry and lift whatever issues, struggles, and burdens that person may have in our midst as we worship God together.

The second component is the stipe which is the vertical bar. This is the bar that was already in place on Golgotha's hill. This represents our one-on-one relationship with God by which God has already established and initiated a relationship with us. This part of the relationship is wonderful because it means we have total access with the Father. In our relationship with Him, we can go directly to God for strength, comfort, and His direction. As a worship leader, this is very critical because in order to lead others into the presence of God, you must stay in tune and connected to God. As long as you're staying connected to him, God will always grant you the grace, anointing, and space to lead His people into His presence.

I encourage everyone of you who lead worship, direct choirs, or sing solos, to not only carry your cross, but to apply the cross you carry as a follower and leader. Carrying and applying your cross will always position you to do what you've been called to do; leading God's people into worship. Your relationship with God is what will keep you relevant as you continue to follow through with His call and mission.

MINISTER UNTO THE LORD
In Chapter 8 we discussed what we are singing, and we learned about the Songs of the Lord. We even learned about the prophetic and how sometimes God will begin to birth something new through us.

Another question I want to propose is who are we singing to? Are we singing to ourselves? Are we singing to the people while we're in praise and worship?

The Bible says in Ephesians 5:19, *"Speaking to yourselves in psalms and hymns and spiritual songs, singing and making melody in your heart to the Lord."* There is definitely a time for us to sing to each other and to ourselves, but ultimately who are we singing to? Yes, we are singing to God. I mean very practically it would make sense. The songs are His. Right? The songs He puts in our mouths are His.

Authentic Worship

Everything relative to melodies, rhythm, and sounds are all His. Anything that's openly and birthed through the prophetic are his. So, as worship leaders we should be singing to him.

"But Samuel was ministering before the Lord —a boy wearing a linen ephod."
~1 Samuel 2: 18

"Sing to the Lord a new song; sing to the Lord, all the earth."
~Psalms 96:1 NIV

When we sing unto the Lord and approach Him with songs of praise, worship and adoration, His presence will come. His presence, through the worship and through the songs will begin to strengthen, encourage, and empower the people of God. This will work every time.

Think about this for a moment. How many times have we failed to apply this? Would you rather beat down the people by telling them, "Oh you can do better than that!" "Come on saints, praise him!" "Come on, he deserves a better praise than that." Does this make sense? We cannot allow ourselves to become coaches, dictators, and bullies during the worship experience. Instead of being so critical to the congregation because you're not getting the reaction you want; Why not simply sing and minister to God? After all, every song we sing should be unto Him and for His glory. Let's encourage the people by blessing God with His songs. The Lord already knows how to deal with His people. He knows what they need before they have any idea. As you sing the songs of the Lord, His presence will come on in and give every individual what they came looking for. It could be healing, a breakthrough, or deliverance. His glory and presence will meet every need as you and the team sing to Him.

"In the presence of the Lord, there's the fullness of joy, at his right hand are pleasures forevermore."

~Psalm 16:11

IT IS NOT A ONE-MAN SHOW
Too often as leaders in worship we can easily start feeling ourselves and we think the worship service is all about me, myself and I. We can easily get caught up thinking it's all

Authentic Worship

about me and what I'm doing but as God's servant today, I have to remind you it's not about you or even what you're doing.

"For it is God that worketh in you both to will and to do of his good pleasure."
~*Philippians 2:13 KJV*

We understand it takes a special grace, anointing, and skill to lead. Just know, at the end of the day, it's not a one man show. Leading worship is a collective effort amongst the team, with one purpose and that's leading God's people into His presence as you sing unto Him. So even if you're leading the song, there's still a joint effort amongst the team. Have you ever seen the movie Drumline with Nick Cannon? Great movie, I might add. Nick Cannon who plays the star role is a talented kid who can play drums. Because of his talent, he's offered a scholarship to play for Atlanta A&T University. However, in spite of his talent, he constantly ran into trouble with the leader of the drums section. Now mind you, he was actually a better talent and better drummer than his leader, but his arrogance cost him to be temporarily suspended and removed from the band. It took him a while to learn what his director had been trying to convey to him, "One band, One sound." We are a team; a comradery with a common goal.

"Then David said, None ought to carry the ark of God but the Levites. For them hath the Lord chosen to carry the ark of God, and to minister unto him forever."

"And it came to pass, when God helped the Levites that bare the ark of the covenant of the Lord… "

1 Chronicles 15:2, 26 KJV

See, the Levites collectively carried the ark of God. Not one person. So consequently, we as a team ought to collectively lead God's people into his presence. Also, I want you to notice what the Levites carried. They carried the ark of God. What is the ark of God? The ark of God represents His presence. Now we already discussed the importance of carrying and applying the cross. Thus allowing us to effectively lead others in the worship experience. Another cross dynamic is carrying the ark of God; His presence. When we come together as a unit, we have a responsibility as leaders to carry the manifestation and

Authentic Worship

presence of God. What a responsibility! What a task! We are blessed my friend to have such a responsibility. I pray that you, your team, and music department won't take it for granted. Let's become the best followers and leaders of worship. So the people will have an engaging experience with God and a personal God encounter. I declare this is a new season for our music ministries. We are going to carry God's glory with His help. I decree there's going to be an overwhelming flow of breakthroughs ,healing, and deliverance. Somebody's son and daughter are going to experience the presence of God like never before. Somebody is going to give his or her life to Jesus Christ. Some backslider is going to come running to God. Revelation, knowledge and understanding is going to increase in every music ministry. New songs and the prophetic is being birthed. The sound of God is being released because we are coming together as a collective to lead God's people in worship the right way. In Jesus name, Amen!!

10

THE G.O.A.T.
(The Greatest of All Time)

<u>G.O.A.T</u>: Greatest of all time.

Quote:
"Who comes to mind when you think of the G.O.A.T. ? Maybe an athlete, actor/actress or singer/song writer. However, from a biblical context the G.O.A.T. is a servant. Someone who is selfless or a person that gives their all for others. Jesus Christ gave His very own life for those that He knew wouldn't accept Him. He became sin for us, just so we would be forgiven of our sins. He became the ultimate sacrifice so that you and I could have a relationship with the Father and enjoy eternal life. Jesus is THE G.O.A.T. without question or debate. We owe Him nothing but worship, honor, and total surrender. Hallelujah!"

~Janee Smaw

To begin this chapter, I think it's very important for us to understand that being a worship leader is more than just one person or persons leading a song during the worship

Authentic Worship

service. Of course, we know within our music ministries, you need singers, a team, certain people who can stand out and lead the people into worship. Now, that's not what I'm talking about. In fact, I can assure you that the conversation Jesus was having with the Samaritan woman was about a general body of believers. Believers from all over the world who would totally dedicate their lives to God. They know that true authentic worship always begins and ends with how we live for Him.

When I think of the true worshippers that Jesus was talking about, I want you to consider them not only as worshippers but as followers of Christ. You cannot worship someone, you're not willing to follow. Think about the disciples of Jesus Christ who followed Him. Even after Jesus went away, His disciples continued the mission He started. It was at that point they became true leaders. Considering the conversation between Jesus and the Samaritan woman. I believe there's a duality amongst these true worshippers that Jesus is conveying to us. These true worshippers who choose to follow, serve, and live for Him would also be the great examples and leaders of worship. Great followers become great leaders and in order to lead you have to be willing to follow. In essence, what Jesus was saying to us is that these true worshippers who are followers will be the true worshippers that will lead.

When I think of true worshippers, I think of individuals who are authentic, genuine, and uncompromising to a fictitious character. This is a pristine collective group of individuals that God will use as a template for other believers to follow. One day, those followers of worship will become leaders of worship. I believe you're one of them. Let's follow and lead!

GREATEST OF ALL TIME
Who is the goat? You know the disciples of Jesus Christ would have debates about who is the greatest in the kingdom of heaven.

"At the same time came the disciples unto Jesus, saying, Who is the greatest in the kingdom of heaven?"
~Matthew 18:1 KJV

For the disciples, This was a big deal to them. In fact, in another passage of scripture the disciples were interested in who can sit on the Father's right and left hand. We all want to

Authentic Worship

have some kind of entitlement. However, Jesus told them you have no idea what you're asking.

Seemingly, this would be similar to the debates that happen all the time amongst sports within the NBA (National Basketball Association). I told you I love sports. So, who's the greatest of all time? Lots of people tag along with Lebron James who's a 3x champion and 4x MVP (Most Valuable Player) and he's still writing history. Then there are those who ride with Kobe Bryant who's a 5x champion and 1x MVP. There's also those who just separate themselves from the good cause they're the best in what they do. Michael Jordan 6x champion and 5 MVP's. He's considered amongst many in the NBA as the G.O.A.T or The Greatest of all Time.

Well saying all that to say, I would be remiss if I didn't share with you the real G.O.A.T as it relates to worship. That would be none other than Jesus Christ crucified. He's the real G.O.A.T amongst us all. In addition, to Him being the G.O.A.T, it would just be a disappointment to share with you the words of Jesus and to not share his experiences, His struggles and issues. I mean come on, talk is cheap, right? I'm looking for somebody that's not only talking it but living it. Jesus is definitely that guy. Let me explain.

Every chapter that has been discussed is all summed up in the life of Jesus. His mission, priority and focus was to fulfill the will of His father. There's no greater worshipper than Jesus. He's the epitome of what true authentic worship really is. Why? Chiefly, what separates Jesus from all of us is not only the fact that He was a living sacrifice as we're supposed to be, but He was the ultimate sacrifice who died for our sins. Remember how we talked about the cross? Jesus carried the cross and laid down His life even while we were yet sinners. See, real worship requires us to make sacrifices. Particularly, when God is expecting you to do something that you don't want to do. Remember when Jesus was in the Garden of Gethsemane? Did you know Jesus didn't have to die for us? Did you know Jesus didn't want to go to the cross?

THE G.O.A.T CONTINUES
Who's the G.O.A.T? Let's make this perfectly clear because another thing about being the

Authentic Worship

G.O.A.T is someone who changes the landscape of his or her field. It's someone who actually becomes a trendsetter and sets the standard for the rest of us to follow. Oh, Jesus did that. He set the standard for all of us to follow. He took 12 guys and the world hasn't been the same. Even with all the different ethnicities, philosophies, and culture, people today are still following Jesus. He's more than a game changer; He's the most influential man and He is all God. Earlier I shared with you that Jesus did not want to go to the cross. Look at what He says.

"Going a little farther, he fell on his face to the ground and prayed, My Father, if it is possible, may this CUP BE TAKEN from me. Yet NOT AS I WILL, but as you will."
~Matthew 26:39 NIV

"And He went a little further, and fell on His face, and prayed, saying, O my Father, if it be possible, let this cup pass from me: nevertheless not as I will, but as thou wilt."
~Matthew 26:39 KJV

Do you see that? As much as Jesus showed compassion, pity, and empathy, He had no interest in dying for us. Yes, He healed the sick, raised the dead and casted out devils. He rebuked the Scribes and Pharisees. He liberated people and gave them hope, but at the end of day, He was not as open with the idea of dying for us.

Gethsemane means "olives pressed." It's the place where olive branches would be crushed by stones, so that the oil could be released. Jesus himself was in that place where His will, His desire and His own idea was crushed. See, when you get to this place of worship, this is about someone's life who has totally surrendered, yielded and reformed to the will of God. Remember, we want to offer ourselves as a living sacrifice, holy and pleasing to God because this is our true and proper worship. What we want is our lives to be pleasing to God for His satisfaction and not our own. Let's take another look at Jesus' prayer.

"Going a little farther, He fell with His face to the ground and prayed, 'My Father, if it is possible, may this cup be taken from me. Yet not as I will, but as you will.'"

Authentic Worship

"He went away a second time and prayed, My Father, if it is not possible for this cup to be taken away unless I drink it, may your will be done."

"So, he left them and went away once more and prayed the third time, saying the same thing."
~Matthew 26:39, 42, 44 NIV

Can you see His act of worship within His prayer? He prayed the same prayer not once, not twice, but three times. He continued to say, not as I will but as you will. See, worship is about what God desires to will through you; your mind, body and soul. Will you worship God by totally surrendering to what He wants? Will you say yes to what He wants to will through you for His satisfaction? Will you choose to follow through with His plan? Worshipping the Almighty God in spirit and in truth is a choice. Will you choose to follow surrender to, and trust him even when things are bleak and seemingly in turmoil? That's the heart of a true authentic worshipper.

Maybe you're going through a Garden of Gethsemane right now. Maybe you're in a place where it seems like different things are being crushed, pressed, and broken in your life. You're right at the point of no return. You just want to run away from the will of God. I'm here to tell you, the struggle is real. Now this is the point where true authentic worship begins. It's when you can say yes to God's will. Can you say yes?

OK, let's turn the heat up some more because if you're saying yes and be a follower of true worship, it's going to require self-denial. It's going to require you to say "NO" to some things that you want to do and yes to things you don't want to do. That's what Jesus did. He said no to himself. He was really saying no to His own preference as He prayed to the Father. Let's just be honest. Who wants to die? I believe that night while He prayed in the garden, there was a worship that rose up in Him. He must've said, "you know what? This isn't about me. This is all about pleasing my Father and what He wants".

What did Jesus do? He went to the cross. He died for us. He gave His life as the ultimate-living sacrifice, so that He could become the primary example of what true authentic

Authentic Worship

worship really is. Jesus Christ is our true leader of worship.

LEAD BY EXAMPLE

Well, there it is., Jesus is the greatest. He is the goat! The Greatest of all time! He is our blueprint, guide, and leader of true worship. Jesus laid a great foundation for us to build on. It's up to us to follow His lead, so that we can become leaders of true worship.

In the same way, there is another person who I feel is necessary to share. This man had never seen Jesus, but he was such a Jesus freak. In fact, he had so much revelation of Jesus Christ, he wrote most of the New Testament. I give you the Apostle Paul. Now this man wasn't the most beloved. Just like all of us, he had his issues as well. For a while he was on the other side of the fence causing havoc and turmoil amongst the church. He was dragging Christians out of their homes and having them persecuted until one day he had an encounter with God. That changed the rest of his life. In addition, to his life, another thing that's interesting about him is he had a similar, yet different situation like Jesus. This man prayed the same prayer three times concerning suffering that would not be removed by the Lord. He's definitely someone we learn, glean, and follow.

Here's why:
"Therefore, in order to keep me from becoming conceited, I was given a thorn in the flesh, a messenger of Satan, to torment me. Three times I pleaded with the Lord to take it away from me. But he said to me, "My grace is sufficient for you, for my power is made perfect in weakness." Therefore I will boast all the more gladly about my weaknesses, so that Christ's power may rest on me."
~2 Corinthians 12:1-10 NIV

See, Paul had a similar different experience as Jesus. Of course, it wasn't to the degree of a crucifixion. However, just like all of us, he had his own personal cross to carry although he prayed three times just like Jesus. While wanting this thorn of suffering to be removed, God tells him "my grace is sufficient." So, what does Paul do? Well, he does exactly what Jesus did. He surrenders to the will of God. No wonder Paul was such an amazing leader. Look at what he says to the church of Corinth.
The Apostle Paul said,

Authentic Worship

"Follow my example, as I follow the example of Christ."

~1 Corinthians 11:1 NIV

Notice Paul said, "follow my example." He could have very well said follow my lead or follow my leadership, but he said follow my example as I follow the example of Christ. Paul knew that if I can follow the example (blueprint, pattern, path) that Jesus lived, I can leave a positive impact on those that are following me; now that's leadership.

See, following Jesus will manually and automatically reposition you in a place of leadership because your life is revealing how a real worshipper should live. So often, we're programmed to believe there's a bunch of steps to a course of action that has to come into place in order to become a leader, but the Apostle Paul said it best, "Follow my example, as I follow the example of Christ."

Unfortunately, it's sad to say that we live in a day and time where leaders are failing to follow the example of Jesus Christ. Consequently, this creates a motto of tainted leadership and unless we follow the example of Jesus Christ, we will continue to fail this now and next generation. There's just no better way than to leave a positive impact on others than through our true example, Jesus Christ. Here are some points we can take away as the Apostle Paul gives one of his protégés some serious wisdom.

"Don't let anyone look down on you because you are young, but set an EXAMPLE for the believers in speech, in conduct, in love, in faith and in purity."
~1 Timothy 4:12 KJV

Notice what things he says to be an example in:

Speech: *Conversation   or maybe a sentence*
Conduct: *Behavior*
Love: *Affection*
Faith: *Confidence*
Purity: *Cleanliness*

Are these things a reflection of true worship and a follower of worship? The answer is yes. All of these things are an example of a follower and leader of worship. I know you've heard me say this before, but I'll say it again. True

Authentic Worship

authentic worship is about living a life that's pleasing to Him. When our lives can emulate a life that's pleasing to God, our lives can show the true essence of being an example.

See, the word *example* comes from a Greek word called, typos tü-pos (that is a model for imitation).

Sometimes my heart is heavy when I think about some of our young people who are misguided, because there's no accountability, responsibility and stability amongst true leaders. Sometimes there's just a lack of role models. If we had some examples and people who are a model of authentic worship, we can duplicate more followers for Jesus Christ. Can I go further? A predecessor has failed if he or she has left nothing for the successor to follow.

For instance:

Predecessor/Successor

1. Moses/Joshua
2. David/Solomon
3. Elijah/Elisha
4. Paul/Timothy
5. Jesus/Disciples

6. Disciples/Us (today's church)
7. Us/Them

There's one common denominator amongst these examples that are shared and mentioned. The predecessor left something behind for the successor to have and utilize for his success as a successor. This should be the role of every true leader. Take a look at these scriptures.

Moses/Joshua
"And Joshua the son of Nun was full of the spirit of wisdom; for Moses had laid his hands upon him: and the children of Israel hearkened unto him, and did as the Lord commanded Moses."
~*Deuteronomy 34:9 KJV*

David/Solomon
"My son, hear the instruction of thy father, and forsake not the law of thy mother: For they shall be an ornament of grace unto thy head, and chains about thy neck."
~*Proverbs 1:8-9 KJV*

Elijah/Elisha
"And it came to pass, when they were gone over, that Elijah said unto Elisha, Ask what I

Authentic Worship

shall do for thee, before I be taken away from thee. And Elisha said, I pray thee, let a double portion of thy spirit be upon me. And he said, Thou hast asked a hard thing: nevertheless, if thou see me when I am taken from thee, it shall be so unto thee; but if not, it shall not be so."

~2 Kings 2:9-10

Paul/Timothy

"He took up also the mantle of Elijah that fell from him, and went back, and stood by the bank of Jordan; And he took the mantle of Elijah that fell from him, and smote the waters, and said, Where is the Lord God of Elijah? and when he also had smitten the waters, they parted hither and thither: and Elisha went over."

~2 Kings 13-14 KJV

Jesus/Disciples

"Wherefore I put thee in remembrance that thou stir up the gift of God, which is in thee by the putting on of my hands."

~2 Timothy 1:6 KJV

Disciples/Us (Today's church)
"I will not leave you comfortless: I will come to you. But the Comforter, which is the Holy Ghost, whom the Father will send in my name, he shall teach you all things, and bring all things to your remembrance, whatsoever I have said unto you."
~ John 14:18, 26 KJV

Us/Them
"And they continued steadfastly in the apostles' doctrine and fellowship, and in breaking of bread, and in prayers."
~ Acts 2:42 KJV

What I really love about these scriptures is the fact that it didn't matter whether it was tangible or intangible. Every predecessor left something behind for his successor to possess. Moses laid hands on Joshua and he was filled with the spirit of wisdom. David tells his son Solomon to listen to instructions. Elijah leaves his mantle with Elisha after being taken away by a chariot of fire and Elisha gains a double anointing at his own request. Paul laid hands on Timothy to affirm his gifts and anointing.

Authentic Worship

Jesus leaves His disciples the comforter which is the Holy Ghost. The disciples of Jesus Christ and the birth of his church in the book of Acts have so many examples, we can follow and apply as a church today. This brings me to number 7 that's left with a question mark. Why? Because that's something we need to ask ourselves. Are we going to leave something behind for this next generation? Are we going to leave behind a legacy for the generations to model and follow when they become leaders?

We have a major responsibility to not only impress those who are coming behind us but leave an impact that will change their lives forever for the good. Whether you're a parent, big brother, big sister, mentor, life coach, instructor, teacher or pastor, live a godly lifestyle that reflects what God is calling for. Create a culture in your space that reflects how God wants us to live. Show and share the message of Jesus Christ. He's the good news that has power to save.

RIGHT NOW!
Who's ready to answer the call of true worship? Jesus said the true worshippers shall

come to worship the Father in spirit and in truth but there's a significant part to this equation of true worship. Please take a look at this.

"Yet a time is coming and has now come when the true worshippers will worship the Father in the Spirit and in truth, for they are the kind of worshippers the Father seeks."
~John 4:23 NIV

Jesus said a time is coming and has now come. Whenever you hear the word "now," that means this very moment. It means without delay or to suggest an immediate time that has already passed. So, for Jesus to make a statement like this, is a big deal. It's a big deal because too often we have been waiting around on God and God is saying, I've been waiting on you. I've been waiting on you to make a move. I've been waiting on you to dig deeper, reach higher, and stretch further to a place and posture of true worship.

Do you think the Samaritan woman waited around to carry on more conversation after her debate with Jesus about worship? Absolutely not! She didn't wait around another second.

Authentic Worship

Remember, Jesus had already spoken to her concerning her multiple husbands and the present man she was living with wasn't hers. This was a woman who clearly had relational issues, but she meets this man named Jesus who offers her living water. She gets her breakthrough. She learns more about worship that totally blew her mind. In fact, she left so fast to go back home, till she left her water pot. She actually forgot why she came to the well in the first place. Immediately, she starts making moves. She goes back to the city and starts telling everyone about Jesus.

When you understand and recognize who Jesus is and what he's already done for you, there's no room for any procrastination. This isn't a thing where I'm going to wait on God and see what he says or see what he does. It's one thing when God impresses upon you to be still and not make any moves but trust him in the process. Yet, it's another thing when God is just waiting on His children to get up from where they are to live and be intentional. After all, true worship is intentional when you're determined to live your life pleasing Him.

With all things considered, you don't have to wait. You don't have to wait for a certain period of time for your life to be perfect. Jesus said the time is now. Yes, right now with your flaws and all. Yes, with the mistakes you've made. Yes, with the present issues going on in your life. Jesus says, right now is the time for the true worshippers to come forth. I believe that person is you. I believe the perfect picture that God wants to see is what He already saw the moment He thought of when He created you. He created you to give Him true worship. Authentic worship!

About the author

Mark Smaw Jr is the foundering pastor of Authentic Worship Church. He has been recognized for creating relevant worship services through "The Living Room series" as an artist. Authentic Worship has been releasing music that encompasses healing, power, perspective and persuasion for people to be found cultivated in a sincere relationship with God. He's been preaching the gospel for twenty-five years and is noted as an accomplished musician and worship leader. His ultimate mission is to usher in as many people as he can into God's presence. Mark has committed himself to the call of true worship. He is also happily married to his lovely wife Janee Smaw. Together they have created such a strong-relentless bond in ministry to lead a generation of true worshippers into the kingdom. In addition to this union, he is a proud father of 5 children; Jazzalyn, Aniyah, Mark III, Jordyn, and Journey.

Resources

The Holy Bible, English Standard Version Crossway, publishing ministry of Good News Publishers, 2016

Holy Bible, New International Version. Zondervan Publishing House, 1984

King James Bible. (2020). King James Bible Online. https://www.kingjamesbibleonline.org

Merriam-Webster.com. 2011.
https://www.merriam-webster.com
(8 May 2011).

The Passion Translation Bible: retrieved from, https://www.biblegateway.com/versions/The-Passion-Translation-TPT-Bible/

www.ingramcontent.com/pod-product-compliance
Lightning Source LLC
Chambersburg PA
CBHW050634160426
43194CB00010B/1668